THE SPELL BOOK OF A WICKED WITCH

MAGIC SPELLS TO CURSE YOUR ENEMIES, HEX YOUR EX, AND JINX THE JERKS IN YOUR LIFE

THALIA THORNE

HENTOPAN
PUBLISHING

Cover design by:

Franziska Haase - www.coverdungeon.com

Instagram: @coverdungeonrabbit

CONTENTS

Get this additional book just for joining the Hentopan Launch Squad.

If you're going to be a wicked witch, you better be prepared to protect yourself.

To get your free copy, scan the QR code below with your camera phone.

INTRODUCTION

This is a wicked book, written by a wicked woman, and since you're reading it, you must be a bit wicked, too.

A well known tenet held by some witches, especially Wiccans, is the Rule of Three. It states that whatever you put out into the world, by actions mundane or magical, will return to you threefold. If you put positive energy into the world it will return to you and bring you joy, and if you put out negative energy with wicked spells, you will reap what you have sown.

I was initiated into witchcraft by a Wiccan coven when I was 17, and I stayed a Wiccan into my early 20s, and lived by their lessons. But by then I had learned much more about the way the world works, about the history of the people in it, and life had taught me other lessons. All actions do have consequences, but it's rarely the aggressor who suffers those consequences.

I had lovers who lied to me, bosses who cheated me, and people who I thought were my friends who turned out not to be. I tried to keep my spells on the side of light, and sometimes they worked, but often the result was to simply banish the offending party from my life. That's not a bad result, but it's not what I really wanted. I wanted justice. I decided I could not play by the rules anymore. I was done. Done trying to fit myself into a box that just made me feel small.

Over the next decade I met other witches, many like myself, who had decided that sometimes the only way to get justice in this world is to take it for yourself. They taught me many things, about magic and life, for which I am eternally grateful. The spells in this book were either taught to me by these witches or are ones I created myself and found to be effective.

Since Christianity spread over Europe, witches have been outcasts. Witches couldn't be allowed to continue practicing, because they worked magic outside of the Church's control, and a woman who could not be controlled was surely wicked. I've found that it's usually the outcasts, those who will not fit into the box that society wants them to fit into, who turn to witchcraft in the modern world. When, in all of history, have the rules ever been written by the outcasts? Never. Not once. The rules are not written for us, and following the rules will not bring us justice.

Many witchcraft traditions have an initiation process. But you don't need a formal initiation into witchcraft. Your real initiation is the one life throws at you. Pay attention to the lessons that life is teaching you, look for the signs from the Goddess, and then take action. If you're not a witch already, consider this book your initiation.

You will have to choose which kind of witch you are. Will you be demure? Will you turn the other cheek, no matter how many times you get slapped?

Or will you be wicked?

PART I: INITIATION

Before you go into battle, you better learn how to swing a sword. Before you start slinging spells, you need to know how magic works. The first section of this book will cover what tools to use, the different types of spells, and foundational witchcraft knowledge.

You will learn about setting up your altar, the elements, oils, crystals, and candles. We will go over why colors are important, the different roots and herbs that you will be using, the phases of the moon and what they mean, and even how to prepare for casting your very first spell.

If you are a new witch, it is imperative that you read this section and do not skip over it. It holds vital information that will help you ensure that your spells are successful. A solid grasp of the basics will help ensure your spells are successful.

THE SHADES OF MAGIC

We've all heard the stories of witches burning at the stake, being drowned in order to prove that they were not witches, flying through the air on broomsticks, or even eating children for dinner. Those witches are awful looking women with long hook noses and warts on their faces with hairs growing out of them. Their fingers are long and pointy, their teeth are sharp, and they are out to get everyone.

Is that what a witch looks like? When you walk through the grocery store, do you know when you walk past a witch? Chances are that you encounter them every day and don't even know it. In fact, your neighbor may be one.

Witches got a bad rap in the past, but today we hear more and more people talking about witchcraft right out in the open. That would have never happened even a hundred years ago.

People are starting to understand more about magic and that witchcraft is not something that makes a person scary or evil. The truth is, you don't have to become "Nancy" from "The Craft." You can start out with small spells and work your way up. Or, if you are ready now, you can jump right in.

The Source of Magic

As you learn the spells in this book, you will find that you need certain ingredients. Most of them will be very easy to find. Don't worry; you won't need the eye of a toad any time soon. While these ingredients help to give the magic more power, the magic does not come from these items.

The magic comes from you. As you sit reading this, all of the magic that you are ever going to need or that you will ever use is already within you. The magic comes from your will and intention, as well as your faith in your own ability and the spell you create.

The problem that most new witches face is that they don't know how to get their magic to work for them. Magic will not work if you do not have a strong desire to manifest the thing that you want. This desire must be backed by deep emotions. If you are nonchalantly trying to cast a spell with no passion and no emotion, very little magic will be put into the spell, and chances are it will not work, or it will be a feeble spell.

Black Magic and White Magic

Most people have heard of black and white magic, but what is the difference between the two? Many people would have you believe that white magic is done by people who have only pure intentions. On the other hand, they believe that black magic is done by those who have evil intentions.

The truth is, there is no black magic or white magic. There is only intention and energy. Some claim that there is white magic and black magic to make themselves feel better about practicing magic at all. They think that as long as they are practicing what they call "white magic," it is acceptable. I want to reiterate that magic is magic no matter what the intention or outcome.

The problem with the idea of good versus evil magic is having to decide what is good and what is evil.

Imagine this; you take heroin away from a heroin addict, causing them great pain and suffering. You know that you could quickly ease their pain, but you choose not to. Are you doing something good by taking the heroin away? Or are you doing something evil by watching them suffer? Who are we to decide?

Magic is about balance. There is always bad in the good, and good in the bad. No matter how good our intentions may be, something bad could happen, and even if we mean for something bad to happen, it could cause something great to happen to someone. Sometimes magic just takes its own path.

You can think about it another way. If you were to cast a "white magic" spell that is said to bring you luck, money, or love, all of that has to come from somewhere. Someone else has to lose those things in order for you to gain them. A little bit of dark in the light. That is how things stay balanced. This is one of the reasons that many people believe that all magic is evil.

No matter what type of magic you practice, it is going to affect another person. A simple luck spell will affect someone else and could even change the entire course of their life.

Because so many people think of "black magic" as evil, it is what people tend to turn to when they are desperate. It is the last recourse for those who have no other solution. Throughout history, witches have been the outcasts of society. They have been oppressed and have not found justice in the traditional way.

The same types of marginalized people are finding themselves attracted to witchcraft today. Today's witches are no different from the witches of the past; they are outcasts, downtrodden, oppressed, and often looked down upon. They may feel desperate, as if they have no other way route to justice. That is where this book comes in.

This book is not going to teach you how to conjure demons or deities. Nor will you learn how to control or kill anyone. The "wicked" spells in this book will help you get justice.

Today, when a witch runs through the fields, it is a much different experience than it was in 1692. As a witch, you no longer have to fear for your life. In fact, you'll rarely encounter any serious judgment from others. You can walk into a store and purchase all the crystals, candles, herbs, and other ingredients you want without anyone so much as batting an eyelash. Imagine what the witches of the past would think about this world we live in today!

2

TOOLS OF THE CRAFT

C andles, crystals, herbs, runes, incense, pendants, and poppets... How many times have you found yourself looking at pictures of all of these gorgeous items online? Maybe you have found yourself on Instagram, dreaming of the day when you will own all of them.

It is important to know that having a massive collection of these items is not necessary, and the size of your collection is not going to increase the strength of your magic.

Let's Start with Elements

As you learn about witchcraft, you are going to hear me talk about elements: earth, wind, fire, and water. These elements are beneficial and essential to all life, but they can also be very destructive. As a witch, you will not only learn to use these elements in your spellwork, but to respect them.

Fire represents activity, passion, risk, creativity, inspiration, courage, impulsiveness, and impatience. (male)

Water represents love, empathy, secretiveness, emotion, feeling, adaptability, and artistic. (female)

Air represents thinking, ungrounded, spirited, questioning, intellect, communication, flighty. (male)

Earth represents materialism, practical, grounded, responsibility, steady, work. (female)

Energy is the fifth element.

Each of the elements corresponds with one of the four seasons, as well as the four directions and a color. Fire corresponds with south, summer, and red or yellow. Water corresponds with the west, autumn, and the color blue. Air corresponds with east, spring, and the color green. Earth corresponds with north, winter, and the color brown.

A Witch's Clothes

The first thing to think about when you are casting spells is the clothes that you will wear. Some people choose to wear robes, others may choose darker clothing or long flowing skirts, and still others simply choose to dress comfortably. Regardless of what you choose to wear, make sure you're able to focus on the spell rather than being distracted by the clothes you are wearing. You shouldn't wear anything constricting. Your clothes should be comfortable and allow you to move freely.

Tools of the Trade

You can be a witch without any tools. You can cast spells by merely chanting. Remember, the magic is already within you. That said, there are tools that can help you along your path to becoming a witch. The items that we are going to cover will merely assist you in casting spells.

Grimoire

Every witch has their own grimoire. It is your own book of spells. In it, you write down how you create your magical objects, such as talismans or amulets. Experienced witches often include how to invoke or summon angels, deities, spirits, or demons. You also write down how you perform your spells and charms. Some people include thoughts about their meditations, their notes, ideas, and rituals. Many witches call this their Book of Shadows.

Candles

There are three different sizes of candles that you will use as a witch; the large pillar candles, the taper candles, and tea light candles. Which size you use will depend on the spell that you are casting. Tea light candles work great for spells that are cast only once, because they burn for a short period of time and then are gone. Pillar candles work well for long-term spells, and taper candles are ideal for use on altars. Candles also come in many different colors, and it is vital that you pay attention to these colors, as the different colors have a great deal of meaning when casting a spell.

- **White** - Breaking curses, purification, healing, regeneration, unity, blessings, improved spirituality, connection with the source of all things, protection. White candles are a great general use color and can be used in place of any other color candle if you don't have one in that color.
- **Black** - Absorb negativity, unblocking, stop bad habits, get out of bad situations, connect to ancestors, honor Death.
- **Yellow** - Intellect and mental clarity, for contacting spirits or other realms, for communication, to honor the element of air, to improve energy.
- **Pink** - Romance, friendship, peace, mental and physical health, healing of the heart, emotional health.
- **Red** - Sex, passion, power, good health and vigor, summon the element of Fire as well as Mars.
- **Purple** - To empower magical practices as well as psychic abilities, divination, astral projection and dream magic, attunement with the higher realms.
- **Gold** - Money, wealth, and success spells. Good luck and good health. Attraction. Summon aspects of the sun. Associated with the masculine of the Divine.
- **Silver** - Prophetic dreams, empower intuition, connect with the astral plane, manifest your dreams, female aspects of the Divine.
- **Blue** - Peace, healing, renewal, calm, protection (both psychic and physical), meditation, dream magic, weather spells, job spells, summon the element of water as well as Jupiter.
- **Green** - Healing, growth, fertility, sensation, money spells,

prosperity, abundance, health, summon the element of
Earth, and the Planet Venus.

- **Orange** - Bring positivity and luck, creativity, attention,
inspiration, attraction, expression, new ventures, opens new
doors.

As you are choosing which spell to cast, you will select a corre-
sponding candle. You may also decide to simply burn the chosen
candle on your altar, which we will talk about a bit later.

Incense

Incense is most often used to represent the element of air. There are
also those who will use incense to represent all of the elements. The
smoke that is created with fire represents the air, the materials come
from the Earth, and the incense is created using water. Incense helps
to create an atmosphere that provides the energy needed to invoke
spirits and to cast spells. The type of incense that I am talking about is
the type that you can buy at the store in the form of sticks or cones.

However, there are other types of incense known as non-combustible
incense. These will usually come in the form of dried herbs that are
either loose or are bound together by a piece of twine. They must be
burned in a heat-proof dish and are used in various rituals and spells.
Sage, an example of this type of incense, is used to cleanse unwanted
energies from the area.

Oils

One thing many people don't know about witches is that they use
essential oils in their spellwork. For many witches, these oils are a

staple of practicing magic. Many witches use essential oils to bless their ritual tools, as well as their crystals, amulets, candles, talismans, and even their bodies. They also use them to create their own incense.

Using oils with candle magic can help dramatically enhance the magic because the oils contain the magical energies of the plants from which they are made. Imagine that all of those magical energies are condensed into an oil and placed in a tiny bottle. On top of that, the scent of the oil affects the mind. It puts us in a different mind frame, which helps us to be more open to the powers that be. The scent of the oil enables us to send for the state of mind that we need to set our intention for our spells.

Because essential oils are so expensive, it is a good idea for you to start with just a couple and then add to your collection as you are able. The great thing about essential oils is that a little goes a very long way.

If you are applying essential oils to your skin, make sure that you use a carrier oil such as coconut oil. Simply mix a few drops of the essential oil with the carrier oil before applying it to your skin.

There are many, many kinds of essential oils used in spellwork, but here are the most common and what they're used for:

- **Cinnamon** - Protection, prosperity, power, love, preservation, money.
- **Peppermint** - Love, cleansing, energy, money.
- **Chamomile** - Whimsy, growth, success, happiness, healing.

- **Orange** - Confidence, prosperity, sun magic, power, self-esteem, growth.
- **Jasmine** - Improved psychic abilities, love, intuition, night rituals, passion.
- **Lemon** - Confidence, purifying, renewal, energizing.
- **Lavender** - Relief of anxiety, cleansing, soothing, beauty.

Later in this book we'll be creating magical oils using herbs and roots, which can be used in various spells to boost their power.

Herbs and Roots

Many of the herbs that grow in the natural world around us contain magical properties, that we can harness in our spellwork. In each spell I'll explain why a certain root or herb is used, so that as you get better at casting you can create your own spells using them.

If you're a practicing witch you may already be familiar with the herbs and roots I use, but may be surprised at the way I use them. I've found that herbs used to create a magical effect can also be used to destroy that effect. For instance, basil is often used in spells to draw money to a person. But basil can also be used to draw money *away* from a person, acting like a sponge. Whether the herb creates or destroy depends on the witch's intent.

Many different roots, herbs, and plants are used while creating these spells. The spells take a lot more than just tossing a bunch of plants or roots together. They have to be adequately mixed. Some of the liquid is used for dressing candles. Other herbs and roots are used for anointing people; some are placed in a bath, and some are used to make tea. It all depends on the intention of the spell. You may even create dusting powders or make sachets to hold the herbs or roots. Mojo bags or honey jars can be created to cause people to change their behavior towards you.

Mortar and Pestle

If you are going to be working with roots and herbs you will need a mortar and pestle. This will allow you to grind the herbs and roots on your own to ensure you have the freshest ingredients possible for your spells. It will also allow you to set your intention while you grind them.

Athame

This is a ceremonial double-edged blade that traditionally has a black handle. You will use it to draw boundaries or sacred symbols. An athame is used to command the magic. It is for magical purposes, not to cut. If cords or other items need to be cut, a boline is used. A boline is simply a white-handled small blade crescent-shaped knife.

Wand

The wand has a relatively similar use as the athame. The wand is used to channel magical energy and helps to contain the power while inviting it and encouraging it, but not commanding it. The wand will represent both the air and the fire elements and can be used to cast circles for rituals and for spellwork.

It is important to have a balance of male and female on your altar, so it is essential to be aware that the wand and the athame are both masculine due to their phallic nature. This is why most witches will choose one or the other. Remember the athame commands the magic, and the wand encourages it.

Altar

Your altar is a very personal thing, so it will differ from one witch to the next. However, there are some guidelines that you should follow. The first thing that you should pay attention to is where you place your altar. Some people want their altar to be in a prominent area where everyone can see it. Others choose to keep it more personal and sacred, away from prying eyes.

The next thing you should consider is how elaborate you want your altar to be. I suggest that you start out with a simple altar and add to it only when you find things that feel right to you instead of adding a bunch of stuff all at once.

Before you set up your altar, think about why you want one. What type of energy do you wish to channel? Why are you practicing witch-craft in the first place? What is important to you about witchcraft? What are your plans for the future? What type of space do you want this altar to be?

Choose the direction that your altar will face. North = Earth, South = Fire, East = Air, West = Water.

Next, choose the things that you want to keep on your altar; for example, I keep Red Jasper, which represents the Earth. It is a grounding stone and promotes balance in life. A vast, beautiful white feather for air. A chalice of water for water and a pillar candle (the flame) for fire. This way, all four elements are covered.

Your athame will draw energy to you. Salt will keep away malevolent intents. Your grimoire. Crystals. If you are adding crystals, make sure you know the energy that they bring with them before you place them on your altar.

It is important not to fill your altar with a bunch of clutter. Everything needs space to breathe. While it may be tempting to load it up with all of the things you love, don't. It will only make it harder on you when it comes time to cast a spell.

What is the altar for? This not just a place to keep all of your items looking pretty. It is where you will cast your spells and say your chants. This is where the magic happens, so it is important to make sure that your altar is in a safe place, away from grabby hands.

It is easy to get caught up in buying the fancy-looking baubles because you want everything to be just right, and it is also easy to believe that you need a ton of money if you want to be a real witch. The truth is that witchcraft doesn't have to cost you anything. After all, they didn't have witch shops 300 years ago! You can look for your ingredients. The wonderful and equalizing thing about witchcraft is that you can do whatever works best for you.

It is important to use your grimoire to write down your spells, rituals, and anything else that you find important. This will ensure that you have it on hand the next time you want to cast a spell.

Every other tool that a witch uses is merely supplemental, and is your choice. You don't have to use any of them if you don't want to, or you can use every one of them. It is best to start small, purchasing one or two, here and there, and then waiting for what you feel calls out to you when the time is right. You will know when it is time for you to create an altar and when you come across an item that needs to be added to it. Remember, not everything has to happen all at once.

3

SPELL CASTING

One of the best things about being a witch is casting spells. There are all different types of spells that you can cast as a witch. Most of the time, when a person casts a spell, it is because they are trying to create some sort of change in their life or in the life of another person.

As a witch, it is crucial that you pay attention to the intention and emotion behind your spells. Once you find your magic, it is vital that you heed your feelings and watch your tongue at all times. You can unwittingly unleash your anger onto someone, causing them more pain than you intended, or than they deserve.

As any witch will tell you, there is no right or wrong way to cast a spell. The process is extremely personal and can be tailored to fit your individual situation. Spells can be very simple or very elaborate; it all depends on you.

The bottom line is that a spell is directed by your thoughts. That means it is vital for you to be focused while you are casting your spells. Make sure that you can visualize every detail of the effect of your spell. You cannot have any doubt that your spell will work.

You don't need a fancy altar to cast your spells. There are plenty of witches who cast spells on the floor or use a simple table covered with a tablecloth. There are also those who keep all of their supplies in a box and use the box as their altar.

Cleansing Before the Spell

Before you cast your first spell, it is important for you to take a ritual bath. This will allow your subconscious to prepare for the ritual. This bath is not just about being clean; it is about relaxing your body and mind in order to prepare you for the casting.

Usually, a ritual bath starts with a shower. Wash your hair and body in the shower and then clean the bathtub before you fill it with water. Fill the tub to the point at which your body will be completely submerged in the water. Then add three full handfuls of sea salt to the bathwater.

You should completely submerge yourself under water three times, and spend some time underwater. You can take your time while listening to music. If your bathtub is not deep enough for you to completely submerge yourself, just sit in the water and pour it over your head.

Pull the plug while you're still sitting in the tub, and watch the water drain; as you watch it, visualize all of your problems going down the drain with it. Step out and wrap your hair but allow the rest of your body to air dry. Do not rub your skin with a towel. This will allow the salt to form a protective layer on your skin.

The Circle of Protection

Once you are ready to cast your spell, decide if you need a circle of protection. Not every spell or ritual requires a circle of protection, but it's a good idea to cast one to protect yourself from any energies that might want to cause you harm or distract you from what you are doing.

Casting a circle of protection is a straightforward thing to do. First decide how much space you will need to complete your ritual or spell. Make sure you have gathered all your supplies and ensure that your area is clean. Use your wand or your athame to draw a circle around yourself and your place of work, such as your altar. Then you're ready to continue with your spell.

Starting the Spell

Once you have cast your circle, if you plan to call upon something or someone for assistance, this is the time to do that. Some call the four corners, North, South, East, and West, others may invoke the elements, and still others invoke specific gods or spirits. What you choose to do is entirely up to you and your beliefs. Some do not invoke anything because their magic is strong enough and needs no assistance.

The Spell Itself

The next step is to speak aloud your intention. Be as specific as you can and use as much detail as possible. Some witches find it easier to write down what they want to say before they begin their ritual, so they don't forget any details. Do not use negative words like "don't." Make sure your words are clear and that you know exactly what you want. It is also important that you do not say, "I want."

Speak out your spell as if it already is, because you must believe that it already is. If you are using candles, light them to represent the transformation that is about to take place. Then move on to your chanting or meditation, and prayers.

Concluding the Spell

Many witches conclude their spells with, "So mote it be," some with, "As I speak it, so let it be," or, "As I say it, so shall it be," or something similar. As you finish your spell, you should give thanks. This does not require any actual words; it is enough to simply feel thankful for your spell working, for the things you have, and for your life. If you do want to speak out your gratitude, however, that is perfectly fine. You should thank the elements, spirits, or any gods that you have invoked and bid them farewell. Make sure that you bid farewell to each of them.

Snuff out your candle if you plan to use it again. Blow it out if you do not plan to use it again. Finally, dissolve your circle of protection by bowing your head and saying, "This circle of protection is dissolved."

As you end your ritual, you may choose to ring a bell or clap your hands to release all of the energies at once.

All of this is done at your altar. Each of these items should be kept at your altar so that when you are ready to cast another spell, everything is right there and ready for you.

Whatever your spell is, make sure that it is within your realm of belief. It does not matter how many crystals or candles you use if you do not believe in the spell. You can chant all night long, but if you do not believe in the spell, all of the chanting in the world will do no good.

Break your spell down into smaller, more manageable spells. For example, imagine that you want to cast a spell to make $500 per day, but you currently only make $125 per day. Chances are that you don't believe you will ever be able to make $500 per day. Perhaps it would be easier to cast a spell for you to make $200 a day and then work your way up.

The first spell I was ever exposed to was when I was six or seven years old. I had a spot of eczema on my face that would not go away. A woman came to me and told me exactly what she was going to do. I had no reason to believe that it was not going to work. As a child, I had all the faith in the world that when I woke up the next morning, that spot on my face would be gone. Of course, when I woke up the following day, the spot was gone. I have used the spell many times throughout my life, and it has continued to work time after time without fail. Why? Because I believe so strongly in it. Just like I believe in that spell, you must believe in yours.

4

CORRESPONDENCES

Witches understand that the world is connected in strange and magical ways, ways that most people are completely oblivious to. We call these connections "correspondences", and we know that these correspondences can affect the outcomes of our spells, in both positive and negative ways. Learning correspondences is like learning to read a group of strangers in a room. What's the mood, what's the level of activity, how am I supposed to behave here and now? You don't wear bright colors to a funeral, you don't talk loudly in a meeting, and you don't wear heels to a beach party.

In the same way, each spell has the right time and place that will help it be more successful.

Moon Phases and Spell Casting

You can cast your spells at any time, of course, but there are better times during the month for certain spells.

The Dark Moon

Also known as the New Moon, the Dark Moon Phase is the best time to cast spells that will bring revenge and justice because this is when frustrations and anger are expressed. It is also a good time to cast spells that will help you attract a new soul mate, or love, or attract positive energy into your life.

This is a good time to set new goals, to tidy up your altar, write new spells, or look up new ones and take your cleansing bath. You might also spend time meditating and thinking about what you want to achieve over the next month.

Waxing Crescent Moon

During this time, you can cast spells that focus on money, business, education, and career. Focus on material gain and long-term spells.

First Quarter Moon

This phase begins about seven days after the New Moon, and during this phase you should focus on your most significant blockages and deepest wishes. The first quarter is when witches concentrate on self-healing and growth. This will allow you to become more aware of your intuition as it develops. During this period, you might also concentrate on abundance, which will enable the right people to come into your life. Cast spells of luck and love. If you are a brand-new witch, this is the time to cast your first spell.

Waxing Gibbous Moon

The Waxing Gibbous, which starts about ten days after the New Moon, is the time for you to relax and observe. Be patient and wait for the Full Moon. You can organize your tools, add to your book of spells, gather your materials, or take time to spiritually cleanse before the Full Moon. This is not the time to cast any spells.

The Full Moon

The Full Moon occurs 14 days after the New Moon, and it lights up the night sky. During the Full Moon, focus on your social relationships, communication, and interactions. It is a good time to deal with your romantic issues but also the time to cast any type of spell that you want with complete confidence. You can use the power of the Full Moon to boost the power of your magic. Rituals are strengthened, and your spells are much more likely to be successful during this moon phase.

The Full Moon is when you can charge your crystals, which you do by placing them outside under the moonlight. After the crystal is exposed to the moonlight for seven hours, bring it inside. Make sure that the crystal is only exposed to the moonlight. Do not leave the crystal outside all night and retrieve it after it has been exposed to sunlight. Sunlight will change its energy.

Waning Gibbous Moon

The Waning Gibbous is the next moon phase, and it is an excellent time to remove all negative energies. This is when you should cast protection and banishing spells to rid your life of any negative situations or problems. You can also do a cleanse and detox, take a cleansing bath or do a bath spell, or focus on breaking a curse, if you feel that someone has placed a spell on you.

Last Quarter Moon

The Last Quarter begins one week after the Full Moon and lasts for three days. This is the time to finish all of your cleansing and rest, and to renew your energy. Focus on removing yourself from any destructive or toxic relationships, stopping any negative habits, and removing negative things from your life. This is also the time to cast spells against enemies or for justice.

Waning Crescent Moon

The last phase of the moon is the Waning Crescent, which begins ten days after the Full Moon and lasts until the night before the New Moon. During this time, you should focus on reflecting and closure. This is not the time to make any decisions or start anything new. Instead, give thanks that another cycle has come to an end and look forward to the beginning of a new one. Spend time looking back at the things you have accomplished over the past month, as well as the mistakes you have made. Think about what you can improve in the coming month. Perform gratitude and relaxation rituals.

If you feel a connection to the moon, it may benefit you to follow the phases and cast your spells according to them. The moon can have a considerable effect on you, so it is imperative to know when you should hold on to the powers and when to release them.

Color Magic

While we did discuss color when we covered candles, there is actually much more to talk about. When it comes to magic, each color is significant. Use colors in your magic in whatever way works best for you. Of course, you don't have to use colors, but the more pieces of magic that you can work into your spells, the more likely that they will be successful.

One of the fastest ways to add color magic to your life is to consume it through food.

Yellow is associated with the sun, and it helps to improve the mood. It is like a burst of sunshine in a person's life. The color yellow helps to improve depression and sadness.

Orange is much like yellow. It helps improve mood and is known to improve writers' block.

Red represents passion, love, and seduction in magic. If you are in a long-term relationship that lacks passion, using the color red in your passion and love spells can help strengthen them, promising many nights of deep passion.

Pink is used for love. It is much softer than red so is not used for steamy sex but for gentle love. Use the color pink if you want to increase the nurturing in your relationship. Use pink to increase your self-love as well.

Purple is used to improve intuition. It is also associated with royalty.

Blue can be used for communication and clarification, but it also brings peace and protection.

Green represents money. It also represents earthly possessions and starting a new business, as well as fertility. Use the color green in your spells if you want to start seeing the cash flow.

Black is a color that some witches will warn you against using. They will tell you not to use black candles because of hexes. However, what you do is no one else's business. Black candles can be used in hexes and curses, but they can also be used to break curses and protection spells.

White is instrumental in magic because it can stand in for any other color, which is good news for those who do not have a lot of money to invest in their craft. It is also great for witches who are just starting out.

The Seasons

December 21st Yule, which is known as the Winter Solstice, is the shortest day of the year, as well as the longest night. It is on this day that witches celebrate the birth of the Sun God. From this day forward, the days begin to get longer. Winter Solstice begins the 12 days of Yule, during which witches spend time respecting the underworld. We focus on warding off spirits and honoring the rebirth of the Sun God. The Winter Solstice is brief, but the celebration lasts for days.

Traditionally, evergreen plants are cut down and hung around the doors and windows of the home. They are used to ward off death and destruction while symbolizing renewal, rebirth, and life. Because these plants never dull, they are believed to have power over death. Holly is brought into the home and soaked in water before being sprinkled onto a newborn to symbolize everlasting life. The red berries of the holly represent the woman's monthly cycle and ties the moon to the Earth.

Mistletoe is cut, but the mistletoe that is used must never touch the Earth. The white berries of the mistletoe represent the semen. Hanging the mistletoe over the doorway protects against evil and storms.

Wreaths are made to symbolize the wheel of the year, as well as the eternal circle of life. They are made with evergreen plants and are decorated with different berries, pinecones, or acorns and are then hung around the home.

Witches will use bells to drive away negative energy and demons. The bells are rung in the morning in order to keep the darkness away.

The Spring Equinox begins on March 21st. On this day, the German goddess, Ostara, is honored. Finally, after spending months in the dark winter, the days grow longer, the sun begins to shine, and the snow begins to melt. Ostara is also known as Eostre, and ancient witches held festivals that centered around fertility and birth. Today these festivals would look more like what we call Easter.

This is the origin of egg painting, as it is a leftover tradition of those who celebrated Ostara, with the eggs symbolizing fertility (as well as the rabbit). Today a witch can celebrate by painting your own sigils on eggs in pastel colors, which are the traditional Ostara colors. When they're done, place the eggs on your altar.

The summer solstice begins on June 21st and is also known as Litha or Midsummer. This is the day when the sun is at its peak. It is the longest day of the year. Everything is filled with life, and we are able to forage or begin harvesting from our gardens. Spending time outside and harnessing the power of the sun is very important to a witch.

Fire is symbolic during this solstice. In the past, huge bonfires were built, and healing herbs were burned to honor the sun and to ward off the darkness. Ashes from a fire can be collected and used in magic, particularly in healing. It is also a great night to cast love spells if you feel like you need a little more love in your life.

The Autumn Equinox, also called the Feast of Mabon, arrives on September 21st. Witches celebrate Mabon by baking goods using the items they have harvested from their garden or for which they have foraged. A feast is prepared with foods like cornbread, squash, corn, and beans. The coven, or family, of the witch all come together and enjoy the meal before going out into nature to appreciate Mother Earth.

In addition to the seasons, there are other important days that a witch needs to know about. Did you know that each day of the week has its very own unique magical power? By knowing what these powers are, a witch will know what spells will be most successful on which day.

Days of the Week

Sunday is named after the sun, and it is a good day to cast spells associated with wealth, divination, healing, success, health, and wealth. As the first day of the week, it is a good day for you to focus on new beginnings and to clear out bad energy.

Monday is named after the moon and is a good day to cast spells that are associated with wisdom, dreams, protection, medicine, prophecy, clairvoyance, and intuition. It is said that on Monday, the astral plane is close to the Earth, and all magic that has to do with spirits is heightened. Water magic or magic involving emotion is strengthened.

Tuesday is named after the Norse god of war, Tyr, and is an excellent day to cast spells associated with protection, defensive magic, sex, gardening, breaking negative spells, and revenge. This is a great day to focus on reversing any hexes that have been put on you, and to block any psychic attacks while fighting off any negativity in your life.

Wednesday is named after Woden, the Germanic god also known as Odin, and it is a good day to focus on settling old conflicts. Perform spells that have to do with luck, fortune, money, communication, business, and divination. Because it is ruled by Mercury and Mercury is a trickster, it is a good day to cast spells that will distract, mislead, and deceive.

Thursday is named after the god of thunder, Thor, and it is a great day to focus on performing spells and rituals associated with wealth, abundance, self-improvement, success, luck, writing, and well-being.

Friday was named after the goddess, Freyja. Venus rules this day, which is a good day to cast spells associated with anything related to love and beauty. You should focus on spells that involve romance, sexuality, marriage, income, relationships, sexual matters, pleasures, and passion.

Saturday was named after Saturn, the Roman god, and is the day that you should focus on your third eye abilities. Cast spells to bind or curse, or to banish or protect. Communicate with your ancestors and other spirits on this day. Your cleansing spells should be cast on Saturday as well. Karma spells, exorcisms, spells to find lost items, habit-breaking, and psychic attack spells should also be cast on Saturday.

Important Dates

Every year there are important holidays that witches celebrate:

Beltane, also referred to as May Day, occurs on May 1st. This is the midpoint between spring and summer. You should focus all of your magic on fertility spells on this day. Witches are known to dance around the maypole on Beltane.

Lammas occurs on August 1st. The first crops of the year are harvested on this day. This holiday is associated with growth and abundance. Some refer to Lammas as Lughnasadh.

Samhain occurs on October 31st. Many people associate Samhain with Halloween, and while it may feel a lot like Halloween, it represents more than just candy and costumes. Samhain marks the Witches New Year, and it is the day when the veil between the worlds is the thinnest. This means it is an ideal time to practice divination to contact your ancestors.

Witches celebrate Samhain by honoring their ancestors and those who have passed. They place a lit candle in a window facing west, in order to guide those souls back home. A table is set for the Samhain feast, and places are left for loved ones.

Turnip or pumpkin carving began because witches would carve sigils into them to ward off evil spirits. It is also believed that by dressing up in costumes and building a bonfire, a witch could scare away evil spirits. Traditionally, treats were exchanged during Samhain for blessings and prayers for those who had passed.

During Samhain, you can decorate your altar in orange, black, purple, and red. Burn sandalwood, patchouli, and myrrh incense: place apples, bones, oak leaves, pumpkins, and cornstalks on the altar.

When the time comes to perform your Samhain Ritual, place pictures of those who have passed on your altar to honor and remember them.

It is easy to see that a lot of today's holidays came from witch tradition and, in fact, are still celebrated in much the same way that witches used to celebrate them. Today, however, those who celebrate these holidays tend to deny that they have anything to do with witchcraft.

Each of the days that we have talked about in this chapter will affect your magic differently. There are specific days when casting certain spells will be easier. That doesn't mean that you can't cast any spell that you want or need at any time. It merely means that your spells will be strengthened on these specific days.

5

TALKING TO THE DEAD

Many people are enchanted by the idea of talking to the dead, and they try it often. You may see it on different "ghost hunting shows." You may see these people trying to speak to the dead through EVP sessions, Ouija boards, and other conduits. There is no proof, however, that any of it is real.

The truth is that you do have the ability to speak to the dead, whether you are psychic or not. Throughout this chapter, I will show you exactly how to do it.

Before we jump into how to talk to the dead, I want to give you a warning. Working with spirits can be very dangerous. As a witch, spirits of all kinds will be drawn to you. This means that the unwanted and wandering spirits will make their way into your personal space as well as your home. These uninvited spirits can be harmless, but many of them can be very dangerous.

It is essential that you become aware of the spirits that are familiar to you and those that are uninvited. Make sure you pick up on those who are uninvited as soon as they enter your space. These spirits can become attached to you or your family, so you should deal with them as quickly as possible.

If you feel that you are not a strong enough witch to deal with these spirits or you fear them, you are not ready to practice any magic that will allow you to communicate with ANY spirit. Never obey orders from a spirit that you would not obey from a person. Spirits are not all-knowing, and you must take everything that they say with a grain of salt.

The dead will communicate with you in many different ways. They may appear before you in the room you are in or communicate with you in your mind's eye, and this is a very powerful experience. However, this takes a lot of energy on their part, and is very hard to do.

Appearing to you in your dreams is much more common, and where the dead are able to speak clearly to you. A few minutes with you can seem like days to them, and they are able to give you important messages that they would not otherwise have been able to share.

When you are communicating with the dead, you may smell a particular scent. This is their way of making themselves known to you. It will be a scent that you associate with them, and that makes you think only of them.

One sure sign that you are communicating with the dead is that you will hear them call your name. You may hear this inside your head or externally. Answer them and let them know that you have heard them.

Simply sensing a presence in the room with you is a sure sign that a spirit is present and is reaching out to communicate. There is a distinct feeling one gets when a spirit is trying to communicate. You can be alone in a room and yet know with certainty that someone is right next to you. You can feel them standing there, looking at you, almost as if they are touching you. Sometimes you may even feel them touch you.

Graveyards

Most witches love to spend time in old graveyards and cemeteries; however, doing magic in cemeteries is a subject that many don't talk about. Is it that they are uncomfortable with death? Are they afraid that people will not take them seriously? Or maybe they fear being seen as practicing "black magic." Practicing magic in graveyards is usually associated with Satanism, hexes, or curses, but this is not at all what is happening.

Cemeteries are great place to practice magic because they are a spiritual place. They also allow you to be close to nature while not being disturbed by joggers, kids, bikers, or anyone else.

A cemetery is a quiet place that holds emotional energy that attracts entities. It symbolizes the region between this world and the next. It is easy to find old cemeteries simply by driving around your community. Many of them have been forgotten.

There are certain graveyard spells in which you will need a specific type of grave dirt. For example, revenge spells call for a person who was murdered, money spells call for a rich man's grave, and a spell to conceive requires a baby's grave. Doing a little research will help you find just the right grave.

While old cemeteries are useful, don't forget about the modern ones as well. Many witches will use graveyard dirt from new graves in their spells and go to newer graves for other tasks.

There are some rules that must be followed when working in a graveyard, and they mainly have to do with showing respect for the spirits there.

- Never point at or photograph the graves.
- Do not step on or over a grave. If you do so accidentally, apologize.
- Never whistle in the graveyard.
- Leave coins on the grave you visit to show your respect.
- If you smell roses when there are none around, it means there is a benevolent spirit near you.

Remember that when you're in a graveyard, you're a guest, and behave accordingly.

Any type of magic can be worked in a graveyard. You can cast love spells as easily as revenge spells. You can also charge your amulets, talismans, and tools.

Gathering Dirt, Stones, and Tree Branches

Often, witches will visit cemeteries simply to gather tree branches, stones, or dirt. There are specific rules that must be followed in the gathering and removal of these items. You cannot take anything that is not given freely, or that has not been bought and paid for.

If you go into a graveyard to collect your items and feel that you are not welcome ,or that you are intruding, simply move on to another cemetery. Bring coins or whiskey with you and leave them on the graves where you find the stones, dirt, or branches.

Using Graveyard Dirt in Spells

Using graveyard dirt in your spells may seem a bit off-putting, but witchcraft has called for it both in ancient and modern times. There are countless rituals and spells that call for graveyard dirt.

Samhain rituals use graveyard dirt to honor the dead. Sprinkle the graveyard dirt around the perimeter of your circle so that your ancestors are included in your ritual. If you want to communicate with the dead beyond the graveyard, you should place some of the dirt in a drawstring bag and leave it with your tarot cards for a complete moon cycle. You will read the cards during the Dark Moon.

You can also use graveyard dirt at a crossroads when you are casting a spell to help you make a decision in your life. Graveyard dirt can be used in the fall in your garden to honor the circle of life and encourage the dead to live again in the form of your plants. There are many more ways to use graveyard dirt. It is beneficial in your spells and should not be overlooked as an ingredient.

Working Magic in the Graveyard

Graveyard magic is not for those who are afraid of haunted houses or cemeteries. It is not something that you should take lightly because there are dark entities, and they will pick up on your fear. Fear will put you at risk. You have to make sure you are protected before you even enter the graveyard.

Begin by casting a protection spell and covering your head before you enter the graveyard. Make sure you're doing the spiritual work, because you do not want anything attaching itself to you.

It is also vital to establish a strong relationship with the gatekeeper, or the person believed to be the first buried in the cemetery. They have been given the job of watching over the cemetery and ensuring that it is kept safe. In the past, sometimes a vagrant or an animal would be the first buried, in order to serve this purpose. If the gatekeeper does not like people, the cemetery will become haunted in order to keep people out. You will quickly be able to tell whether or not you are welcome in the cemetery.

Bring goodies each time you visit the cemetery. Spend time cleaning up the headstone of the grave that you intend to use, make sure that you leave no trash behind. Build rapport with the dead before you begin practicing magic. You can do this by spending time talking to the spirit and by giving them gifts.

How do you know what grave to use? Allow your intuition to guide you to the right stone. As you stand in the middle of the graveyard, it may seem a bit overwhelming. So many stones around you, and you have no idea which to go to. Ask for a sign, and you will receive one. Walk around the graveyard until you feel the pull to a specific grave.

Once you have chosen the grave and have built a relationship with its inhabitant, you can begin casting your spells. This does not have to be a long process. In fact, it can be done fairly quickly. As long as your intuition is telling you that the spirit is willing to allow you to cast your spells on their grave, you can. On the other hand, if you get the feeling that you are not welcome, find another grave. Never cast a spell on a grave where you feel unwelcome.

After you have finished casting your spell, make sure you clean everything up. Do not leave anything behind. Ensure that the gatekeeper will welcome you back when you want to return.

Thank the person whose grave you used and say goodbye to them and to the gatekeeper. When you walk out of the graveyard, verbally state that no one is allowed to follow you, and everyone must stay in the cemetery. Make it very clear that no one is allowed to attach themselves to you.

When you return home, it is vital that you do a cleansing. Even though you told the spirits not to attach themselves to you, it is possible that you carried negative energy home. You must take a spiritual bath to clean yourself.

To your bath add a handful of salt, five drops of lavender oil, 15 drops of lemon oil, 10 drops of bergamot oil, and two drops of cinnamon oil, along with a splash of vodka. Clean your body top to bottom in order to push all of the negativity away from you. As soon as you are clean, get out of the water. This is not a bath for soaking in.

This mixture is called Florida Water. You can purchase it already prepared or you can prepare it on your own in advance. It is known as a perfumed spirit. It is incredibly inexpensive to make but very useful.

What Happens if You Don't Follow These Rituals?

Not following the guidelines I've given you in this chapter about entering and leaving a graveyard can lead to severe consequences that can last a long time. Spirits can attach themselves to you and follow you home. Once in your home, they can make themselves comfortable and cause many disturbances that could affect your family. Witches might find themselves in situations that they don't know how to handle and might have to spend a long time looking for help.

The easiest way to avoid all of this is to follow the guidelines that you have been given in this chapter. That is, unless you want to live in a haunted house and lie awake listening to all the things that go bump in the night.

6

DIVINATION

Divination is the ability to foresee or predict the future or to be able to gain some insight into a specific situation or question by practicing different types of rituals. Divination is a great way to understand what will happen if you do not change the path you are currently on.

Divination means connecting to the divine. Many believe that this means connecting to a mystical being, while others believe it means connecting to a deeper, more divine part of the subconscious. I believe that divination just shows us the connections that already exist in the world, but are simply undetectable using our normal senses. What you choose to believe is up to you.

Divination is something that you will come to rely on once you learn how to practice it correctly. From tarot cards, runes, pendulums, crystal balls, and more, you will find that divination offers you a new perspective in your life.

Using Divination Before a Spell

I always like to use some form of divination before I cast any spell, because it helps me determine which spell will work best for my specific situation. Divination also helps witches to know if we need to do multiple spells and if we need to create a plan to do long-term spells.

Divination also allows us to find out if the spirits around us support our spells. If they do not, there is no point in casting them. When we have the go-ahead from the spirit world to cast a spell, we know we are not wasting our time or energy, and that we are on the right path.

Most people who practice divination do so for themselves. If they use their skills for someone else, it is only for a few close friends. Even if what you find out from divination is not pleasant, it is better to know than to be ignorant of this information. As with all other magic, it is important to remember that the magic is not in the object or the type of divination that you are using, but is within you and your relationship to the tool you use.

Tarot Cards

I remember when I purchased my first pack of tarot cards. They were beautiful, and I practiced reading them for hours. Soon I began to understand how to use them, and I became really good at it. It wasn't long before I realized that anyone can become good at reading tarot cards.

The problem is that there is so much information out there about reading tarot that it can quickly become overwhelming. It doesn't have to, though. The truth is that the best way to learn to read tarot cards is with hands-on practice, but a little studying never hurt anyone. That's why I want to provide you with a foundation that you can build upon.

The first step is to choose your deck. There are hundreds of different types of decks available, and it can be a little daunting to figure out which deck is the right one for you. However, there are a few tips you can follow to ensure you have chosen well:

- Make sure you get a full deck of 78 cards.
- Focus on any pack that grabs your attention.
- Buy your own pack. Some witches feel that tarot cards must be gifted to really work, but that is absolutely not true.

Once you have brought home the perfect deck, you have to learn how to charge them and protect them from negative energy and physical damage. Begin by consecrating your deck by burning incense around it. This will protect it from negative energy. Next, wrap your deck in a silk scarf, then place it in a cloth bag with a drawstring and finally in a small box with a lid.

The goal is to make sure that your deck is protected from damage and not scattered all over the house. This will also ensure that if you want to take them with you somewhere, you'll have a carrying case, of sorts. You may want to place them under your pillow for a few nights before you use them so they can absorb your energy.

Tarot cards are known to absorb the energies around them, so if you have a lot of negative people coming into your home, your cards could absorb this energy. To prevent this, place a quartz crystal with your cards. The crystal will absorb the energy instead of the cards. Many witches will not allow others to touch their cards, to ensure that their energy is not absorbed by the cards.

Don't be afraid to try different decks. If you don't feel connected to your deck or you just want to try out other decks, go ahead. If you don't feel connected to a deck, don't worry, you will find your deck when the time is right.

Once you have found the right deck, it is time to have some fun. You will start to learn how to read your cards. Your deck is going to come with a book that will tell you what each card means, but how do you know how to apply these meanings?

When you first get started, there is nothing wrong with reading your tarot cards by the book. You can do this until you begin memorizing their meanings. Once you remember what each card means, you will start to intuitively read them. You should pay attention to the messages and images from the cards. Look at them and see if they are interconnected before you give the reading.

Sometimes it might seem that the cards aren't making any sense. If that happens, reshuffle them and lay them out again. If they still don't make sense, consider recharging or consecrating them again.

Using a Crystal Ball

When people envision someone using a crystal ball, they usually picture a fortune teller in a colorful headscarf waving her hands over the ball to predict the future. That's not really how it works. Using a crystal ball is called scrying, and it takes time and a good deal of practice to learn. Like anything else in life, practice makes perfect.

One assumption made about crystal ball gazing is that images appear in the ball. When one looks into a crystal ball, and doesn't see anything, they assume that they don't have the ability to use one or that the ball doesn't work. Because of this, many crystal balls end up becoming nothing more than an accessory for many witches.

The truth is that the images you see in the ball are in your mind's eye. It may seem like they are in the ball, which is why you must remain focused on the ball while you are gazing, but the images are being seen only by your third eye. If you've ever done intensive meditation, and seen images or symbols, you'll be familiar with this process.

When you're ready to begin, hold your crystal ball for a moment and take a deep breath. If there is a specific question to which you need an answer, you will ask this question in your mind. If you don't have a specific question in mind, you can request to be shown something that will be helpful to you.

Next, place your crystal ball on its cushion or stand and gaze into it. It is very important that you stare into the ball without looking away. Try not to blink but instead hold your gaze as long as possible, even if your eyes become unfocused. A mist will begin to form over the ball, but it will quickly clear, and you will begin to see images.

Don't try to interpret what you are seeing as you are seeing it. This will only break your concentration. Instead, wait until you have seen all the images. Once they start to fade or the mist returns, you can relax and look away. Write down the images that you saw so that you can interpret them later.

When it comes to interpreting the images in a crystal ball, you must remember that they are symbolic. Consider how these images relate to your current situation. Learning how to interpret images can be a little tricky at first, but it gets easier as you spend more time doing it. While you are gazing, you may even hear words that are associated with those images. This is your subconscious helping you, and it should not be ignored.

Think about how the images make you feel when you see them, how they relate to what is going on in your life, and if they cause you fear or if they support you.

Scrying also allows you to spy on other people. By focusing on another person, images will appear in the crystal ball that will allow you to learn more about that person and your relationship with them. Again, it is important to remember that what you see is not what is actually happening but is instead being produced by your intuition. It's information your subconscious has been trying to get you to acknowledge.

Using a crystal ball can be a lot of fun, and it can open your eyes to what is going on around you. I use my crystal ball when I believe that someone is being less than honest with me. We all have times when we question those around us, and scrying is a great way to get some clarity about who we should and should not trust.

Using Pendulums

The use of pendulums in divination has been around forever, and is something that almost every young witch tries. I couldn't have been more than 10 years old when I first started trying pendulum magic because it is one of the easiest ways for a witch to gain information.

I remember sitting in a circle with all of my friends as a little girl and using one of my necklaces as a pendulum and asking questions. Back then, it seemed like nothing more than a game that we had made up, something fun and strange as we watched the necklace change direction. Years later, I know it is much more than that. Many witches find that the "games" they played as a child were actually preparing them to use magic later in life, and using pendulums is often one of these "games."

One example of using pendulums is a game often played at baby showers. The mother's wedding ring is put on a string and held over her belly. According to lore, depending on how the pendulum swings, you can tell if the baby will be a boy or a girl. This is pendulum divination.

A pendulum is simply an item suspended by a string or a chain. You concentrate on a question and then read the way the pendulum swings to determine your answer.

There are some witches who are afraid to use magic tools. They believe that the tool is powered by an entity, but you do not have to worry about this. The pendulum does not have any power of its own, and there is no spirit controlling it. All of the magic is coming from within you. The information you receive comes from you tapping into the universe and allowing the knowledge to flow through you. While we already have the knowledge inside of us, it often becomes jumbled in our minds. The pendulum merely allows us to filter out all of the mess and acquire the information we're looking for.

The pendulum will only have the power that you give it. You are pouring your own energy into it and creating a psychic connection with it. Without the power that the pendulum gets from you, it can do nothing.

How to Use a Pendulum

First find the pendulum that you plan to use. This can be a necklace you already have, or you can create your own. Use your dominant hand to pinch the top of the chain or string with your forefinger and thumb, resting your elbow on the table.

Tap the pendulum with your other hand to ensure that nothing will stop it from moving and that nothing is in its way. Once you know there is no friction on your fingers and everything is moving freely, focus on your question. Usually, the question will have a simple "Yes" or "No" answer. As you gain more experience, you can put a chart or a map on the table under the pendulum in order to find an answer. It is also a good idea to record your reading so that you don't have to remember all the information you are given.

Before you use any pendulum, you will need to cleanse and consecrate it. This will ensure that any past associations are removed. This is very important, no matter what use to create your pendulum.

It is also important to do a preliminary test. Ask the pendulum some questions to which you already know the answer. If the test fails, don't worry; cleanse the pendulum again by running it through incense smoke or soaking it in saltwater, depending on what material it is made of, and then charge it by leaving it under the full moon all night.

Once the pendulum has passed the preliminary test, be sure to keep it in a safe place. Do not allow other people to handle it because that can interfere with your connection to it. Use the pendulum regularly in order to better connect to it.

Using a pendulum is an ideal way to start with divination. Anyone can do it, and it can give you a lot of confidence in your magical abilities. There is nothing scary about pendulums, and chances are you have already used them at some point in your life.

7

PLAYING WITH DOLLS

W hen most people think of dolls and witchcraft, they think of Voodoo dolls, pins, needles, and a lot of torment. Of course, you can use dolls to bring harm to your enemies, but that is not the only reason that these dolls are created. What many people do not know is that the pins stuck into the dolls do not always cause pain. Some can bring blessings, power, wealth, and happiness to the person that the doll represents.

When witches use dolls, we call the poppets. Poppet, which means sweet little thing, was used as a term of endearment and was often used to refer to a child.

The doll that we call a poppet originated in Europe is instead for sympathetic magic. Poppets are used as physical representations of the person you want to affect in your life. Hair or nail clippings may be incorporated into the poppet, and writing the person's name on the poppet is also a common practice.

You can create poppets to represent a person or a thing and this poppet can contain different items that belong to that person. Once the poppet is made and has been charged, any action that you perform on the poppet will cause a similar reaction to the person it represents.

Poppets date back to ancient times when they were believed to be used to bind deities in villages or homes. Today binding spells are more likely to be used on a specific individual to stop them from hurting other people.

Creating a Poppet

You can create a poppet from all types of different materials, including corn husks, paper, wood, mud, fruit, wax, grass, roots, grain stalks, or clay. They can be dressed and stuffed with stones or herbs or other magical items as well as personal items that belong to the person for whom the poppet is intended. This could mean that you dress the poppet in clothing made from a material that was worn by the person, or that you stuff some of their hair or nail clippings in the poppet. People have even been known to add bodily fluids such as saliva, semen, or blood to poppets. Whatever you use, it is important that the poppet and the person it is intended for are linked as much as possible.

You can make your poppets as elaborate or as simple as you like. However, you do need to take the time to learn as much as you can about the person they will represent before you determine the reason for the poppet. Will the poppet be used to bind, heal, harm, or curse the person? The possibilities are endless, just like spellwork, but you must know what your goal is in order to achieve it. The more work you put into your poppets and the more elaborate they are, the more potent your spell will be.

Just like any other magical tool, your poppet will need to be consecrated once it is made. You will need to name your poppet (give it the same name as the person for whom it was created), and you should infuse it with your energy and intention. This can be done by breathing life into the poppet. Simply place a straw at the poppet's mouth and breath into it, while keeping a clear picture in your head of the person the doll represents. This will allow the poppet to take on a life of its own and will activate the spell.

Your actions will depend on the type of spell you are working on, whether it be to harm, bind, curse, or heal. The poppet can be pierced with pins, nails, or other sharp objects to cause pain, just like a Voodoo doll. You can use cool water to cool it off, heat it with fire to cure fevers, or bind it with cords to restrict movement or work a binding spell.

Once you are finished with the spell and the poppet and have achieved your goal, dismantle it and dispose of the ingredients appropriately. It is very important to make sure that any link between the ingredients and the person has been broken.

Commercial dolls or toys can also be used to create poppets, and honestly, it's just easier than making one from scratch. You'll want to find a doll that looks as much as possible like the person you want to affect, and then modify the doll to match the target even more. For instance, these dolls can be dressed in clothing that is sewn from the person's clothing. If the doll has hair, you can braid some of the person's hair in with the doll's. All of this will create a long-lasting link to the person. You should create the strongest connection possible, just like with any other poppet.

8

TYING PEOPLE IN KNOTS

K
not and cord magic is a very versatile tool that you can use in many of your spells or that you can use alone. It allows you to cast spells that are extremely powerful while tying those who are attacking you, simply by using a length of cord.

You can use knot magic with almost any spell; curses, bindings, healing, protective spells, luck spells, and prosperity can all be done with knot magic. In the past, knot spells were only associated with elemental magic or with weather spells. However, today witches use it with all of our spells.

What type of knot am I talking about? Chances are you're imaging a giant knot made of thick rope. Don't worry; there is no magical type of knot to learn. Any type of knot will work. If you are working on a complicated spell, you may decide that you want to use a more ornate knot, but you don't have to use any specific type.

Are there downfalls to knot spells? Unfortunately, yes, there are. Because the knot is the representation of your spell, if it is untied or broken, your spell will be broken. Some witches do not always see this as a drawback, though. It gives you the option to break the spell easily if you need to.

Usually, you'll use string or rope for knot spells, but you can get creative with it. You could use floss, wire, scarves, vines, ribbons – anything you can tie.

How it Works

Cords can be used in a lot of different types of magic. Cords can be used to focus energy, to bless, to carry amulets or charms, and cords of different colors have symbolic value.

Binding is one way to use knotting and cord magic. Wrap the cord around the object that represents who or what you want to bind. This could even be a poppet that represents a person in your life. Once you have wrapped the cord around the person, tie your knot and speak your spell.

Cooperation is another way to use knotting and cord magic. When you want specific people to cooperate with you, each person needs a length of cord cut for them. Each length of the cord should be named after the specific people (one of whom is you) or the situations where cooperation is needed. As you focus all of your energy on the cooperation that you want, you should begin braiding the cords together and tying them at the end. Take this braided cord with you where you need it. For example, if cooperation is needed at work, that is where you should keep this knot.

Joining and releasing is an excellent example of knot magic. Imagine that you are job hunting. You can use one cord to represent yourself and anther to represent the job you want. Tie the two cords together securely. When you get the job, if you ever decide that you are ready to leave, simply disconnect the knot.

Love and friendship knots are also possible. During some marriage ceremonies, people prepare ribbons or cords that represent the bride and the groom. These two cords are tied together, showing that the two have become one. You can do this outside of a marriage ceremony as well. We also share friendship bracelets with our friends from a very young age, and you'll be surprised to hear that this is also cord and knot magic. The color of the cord reflects how you feel about the person, and the exchange of these cords binds the two of you together.

You can also create luck cords. Use colored beads to create your luck cords. Start with a sturdy piece of string and tie beads to it. As you tie each bead, recite an incantation. For example, you may use a green bead for money luck or a pink one for love and use incantations for those specific areas of your life. Wear this cord regularly so that it will bring luck into those areas of your life.

There are so many other ways that you can make cords and use knot magic. The possibilities are endless, but it is up to you how you use knot and cord magic in your life and in your spells.

The color of your cords, just like the color of your candles, will affect the magic. If you want an all-purpose cord, look for a neutral tone, such as a plain rope. If you use the colored cords for their symbolic value, here is what the colors mean:

- **Black** stands for wisdom, protection, dreamwork, banishing, grounding, and introspection.
- **Brown** stands for the Earth element, building, and focus.
- **Blue** represents the water element, peace, devotion, joy, honesty, and forgiveness.
- **Gold** represents success, luck, charm, well-being, and justice.
- **Green** represents garden magic, physical health, luck with money, prosperity, and creativity.
- **Lavender** stands for learning, peacefulness, and intuitiveness.
- **Indigo** represents divination, spirituality, and psychism.
- **Orange** stands for justice, motivation, self-awareness, and goals.
- **Purple** represents leadership, mediumship, freedom, and improved luck.
- **Pink** stands for self-love, romance, nurturing, and gentle love.
- **Red** represents passion, sexuality, positivity, action, the fire element, motivation, and health.
- **White** represents purity, cleansing, spirituality, honesty, and can be used as a substitute for any other color.
- **Yellow** stands for focus, memory, inspiration, joy, self-trust, and the air element.

New witches enjoy knot magic because it is simple, and anyone can tie a knot. When you tie a knot while casting a spell, you are placing something within that knot. While some of these knots will be used for binding and will remain fixed for long periods of time, others will be released when you are ready.

9

DISPOSING OF THE REMAINS

W orking a spell can take time, and once the spell is finished, you are left with the remains. Many witches find themselves wondering what they are supposed to do with all of the remnants. You can't just keep everything and let it pile up in your home, but you also have to be careful not to undo your spell by incorrectly disposing of the remnants.

What is a witch supposed to do with all of the leftovers from all of the spells they have been working on? It is very important that you take the time to dispose of your spell remnants properly. There is a "don't throw it away" rule that witches follow when it comes to their spell remains.

There are times when you can reuse some of your remnants. If you are working a spell with a vigil candle, for example, you may be able to use the glass in a later spell. In order to cleanse this type of item, I would bury it in a large container of salt for 30 days and then place it in blessed rainwater for five days before reusing it. I would never reuse any item that was used in a banishment, hex, or return-to-sender spell.

So, what are you supposed to do if you can't reuse your items? The first thing to think about is how we use the elements when we do spellwork. We can use the elements to dispose of the remains as well. That's right, Mother Nature can help us construct our spells and also get rid of the remains. However, the elements will not always provide a way to dispose of all that we use. This is when we have to be a little creative.

Let's talk about the easiest and most common ways witches get rid of the remains of their spells.

Fire and air are probably the most common method of getting rid of remains because the fire can burn almost all of it, the smoke is lifted into the air, and the ash is carried away by the wind. You can use a fire pit, a wood-burning stove, or make a fire specifically for burning your remnants. Some witches will tell you not to burn your remnants or advise you to only burn the remnants of hex workings. They believe that burning the remnants sends the spell away. If you believe this, you should only burn remnants of items of spells related to ridding yourself of something rather than drawing something to you.

Water is another way to get rid of the remnants of your spells; however, all of these remnants have to be safe to release in water, which means they must be biodegradable and natural. The waters you use can be disposed of this way, as well as other natural items such as dirt and sticks. You can use natural water sources like creeks, streams, and rivers to dispose of remnants from protection, cleansing, healing, abundance, and fertility spells. You can flush some of your remnants as well. For example, if you have remnants left from removing a hex, you should flush them (if they are biodegradable) because this represents you symbolically flushing the hex from your life. It is essential to make sure that everything is environmentally safe before you put it into the water.

Using the Earth is another way to dispose of remnants. Burying remnants is a great way to get rid of leftovers from success, protection, abundance, and prosperity spells. These spells usually work best if you bury them on your property. Because the Earth strengthens and stabilizes the spell and allows it to work over the long-term, burying it helps to ensure that the spell remains permanent. It is essential, of course, to make sure that you bury the remnants in an area where they will not be dug up.

Some witches will bury the remains of hex-work, but most of these spells require this to happen in a graveyard or at a crossroads. Sometimes you will be required to bury the items at a location that is significant to your spell. However, you must be very careful that you do not get into legal trouble when you do this.

Disposing of the remnants of your spells is a ritual in itself. These rituals can make you feel empowered and can bring you closure at the end of your spells.

However you choose to dispose of the remnants of your workings, make sure you do it in a way that provides you with the most favorable outcome for your spell. You don't want to put all of that work into your spell and then ruin it by incorrectly disposing of your remnants!

PART II: THE SPELLS

You're probably excited to have made it to the second part of this book, the spells. Maybe this is the entire reason you picked up this book. If so, don't worry, I know you'll be pleased with the upcoming chapters.

Throughout the next chapters, you will find the spells that you're looking for. Each chapter will start with a small introduction explaining the spells in that chapter. Then we will move on to the actual spells. The spells are easy to perform and the ingredients easy to find. Since you've read the first part of this book and learned all about witchcraft, none of these spells will be hard for you to do.

Are you ready to start getting your revenge? Let's begin with some petty revenge and see how much trouble we can cause.

10

PETTY REVENGE

You no longer have to be at another person's mercy. If someone has been causing you problems in your life, it is time for you to start fighting back. These petty revenge spells will help you do just that.

These revenge spells are powerful, and you should only use them on a person if you are sure of their guilt. If a person has hassled you, if you know the person deserves it, or if you are tired of the way they treat you, these are effective spells for you to cause them to suffer some of your wrath.

Petty revenge spells will allow you to home in on the person causing you problems. They will cause that person to suffer discomfort in their lives, which will take their focus off of you. Remember, before you do any revenge spell, make sure you do a protection spell first.

Agony of Acne Curse

Sometimes you don't really want to do a lot of harm to someone, but you want them to suffer just a bit. This is an excellent spell for someone who is exceptionally vain or who has said something unkind about the way you look.

WHEN TO PERFORM THE SPELL

On a Friday or during a First Quarter moon

HOW LONG IT TAKES

10 minutes

WHAT YOU'LL NEED

- A black marker
- A black candle
- Heat-proof dish
- A picture of the target
- ½ tbsp of chicory powder – to strengthen a curse

STEPS

1. Begin by placing the picture of the person in the dish.
2. Using your black marker, place a few dots on the person's face to represent pimples.
3. Sprinkle the picture with the chicory powder.
4. Light the picture on fire and say:

You have blemished my reputation; now your face will be blemished.

5. Repeat this until the picture and chicory are entirely burned up.

6. Light the black candle and allow it to burn completely.

You will soon see blemishes begin to appear on the person's face.

Tangled Tassels Jinx

This is another fun little spell that will make someone suffer a bad hair day. While it might not cause them a lot of suffering, it might be enough to give you a giggle, knowing that you are the reason for it. It is an especially fun spell when you know they have an important meeting or a big date that night.

WHEN TO PERFORM THE SPELL

On a Wednesday or during a Last Quarter moon

HOW LONG IT TAKES

20 minutes

WHAT YOU'LL NEED

- A bit of the person's hair
- A black candle
- Weeds
- Twine
- A heat-resistant plate

STEPS

1. Use the twine to tie together the person's hair with the weeds.
2. Place the hair and weeds on the plate and light them on fire. As it burns, say this:

Your hair will look like nasty weeds,
Crazy and wild it will be
Uncontrollable for everyone to see
All because of what you did to me.

3. Once the hair and weeds have burned, light your black candle and allow it to burn until it goes out on its own.

The following day the recipient will have a terrible hair day.

Dragon's Dream Spell

Giving a person terrible dreams is a slightly stronger spell than the previous two. It will take a little more magic than does giving someone a bad hair day or a pimple, but its effects will last longer as well. This spell should be used with care and not sent to an innocent person, however, those who deserve it will suffer in their sleep.

WHEN TO PERFORM THE SPELL

At night, on a Monday or during a Dark moon

HOW LONG IT TAKES

30 minutes

WHAT YOU'LL NEED

- One black candle
- Dragon's blood incense
- Charcoal
- Dried mugwort - used to increase psychic attacks
- A piece of white fabric
- Heat-proof dish
- A black marker

STEPS

1. Begin by drawing three circles of different sizes on your fabric. In the smallest circle, draw an x. Place your heat-proof dish with your charcoal on this x.

2. Light the charcoal. Once it is burning, place a pinch of the mugwort and a piece of the Dragon's blood incense on the plate.

3. When all of this begins smoking, light the black candle. As the smoke begins to rise, picture it floating to your target while they sleep. It will bring them nightmares. Repeat their name as you visualize the smoke floating to them.

4. After several minutes of concentrating and chanting the person's name, extinguish the charcoal and place the candle on the x. Leave the candle on the x until it burns out.

The person who has been bothering you will begin having nightmares the following night, and these will continue for the next three days.

Smell Like a Corpse Curse

There is nothing more rewarding than making someone stink just as bad as their attitude does, and the way to do that is with this spell. No matter how much deodorant or cologne they put on, they will not mask the stench that follows them around. Of course, that means that you have to work with some smelly ingredients but don't worry, it will be worth it.

WHEN TO PERFORM THE SPELL

On a Tuesday or during a Waning Gibbous moon

HOW LONG IT TAKES

30 minutes

WHAT YOU'LL NEED

- Dried corpse flower
- A thumbtack
- A white candle

STEPS

1. Place the candle on top of the person's picture.
2. Sprinkle the dried corpse flower around the candle.
3. Stick the thumbtack in the side of the candle.

Light the candle and recite this:

It's time for you to grow

It's time for you to mature
Until then, you will suffer
And smell like the bloom
Of the corpse flower.

4. Repeat this nine times and then allow the candle to burn
out on its own.

The corpse flower smells like rotten fish. If you cannot get your hands
on the corpse flower, you can choose any other herb, plant, or flower
that has an unpleasant smell.

Oppressing Stress Hex

Stress and anxiety are no laughing matter, but if someone is causing you to suffer from them, they deserve the same in return. With this spell, you can let the person know just what they have been putting you through. This spell creates something called a Witch's Jar, which is just a type of container for a long-term spell.

WHEN TO PERFORM THE SPELL

On a Saturday or during a Waxing Crescent moon

HOW LONG IT TAKES

1 hour

WHAT YOU'LL NEED

- A glass jar
- Rusty nails
- Cemetery dirt
- A black candle
- Black mustard seed – to cause stress
- A piece of paper

STEPS

1. Focus on your goal as you visualize the person on whom you want to take revenge. Write the name of the person on the piece of paper and place it inside the jar.

2. Add the cemetery soil, the nails, and finally the black mustard seed.

3. Place the candle in the jar, ensuring that it will stand on its own. You can melt a little of the bottom to secure it to the jar. Repeat the following 30 times:

I am right,
You were wrong
You will no longer enjoy the light
Your suffering will last long
Stress and pain
The reason you can't explain
Anxiety will come
The emotions you won't numb.

4. Allow the candle to burn out.

5. Place the lid on the jar and bury it as close to the person's home as you can.

The Hateful Heart Hex

Nasty people call for nasty spells, and sometimes nasty spells call for nasty ingredients. For this spell, you'll need the heart of a chicken. You didn't think being wicked would be easy, did you? Consider this one a test of your resolve.

Don't worry, you don't have to go cut it out yourself. You can simply request it from your butcher. If they give you a funny look, just tell them it's for an Old World dish. Ingredients like this help to make the spell stronger and last longer. That is precisely what we want when we are dealing with particularly nasty people.

WHEN TO PERFORM THE SPELL

During a Dark moon

HOW LONG IT TAKES

1 hour

WHAT YOU'LL NEED

- A sheet of paper
- A black marker
- Five black candles
- Myrrh incense
- The heart of a chicken
- Twine

STEPS

1. Begin by casting your circle. Place your five black candles around your circle and light them.

2. Light your incense.

3. Write the name of the person you want to curse on the sheet of paper. Raise your paper above your head and say this:

All the hate I have you, now feel for yourself.
All the anger I feel for you, you now feel for yourself.

4. Allow all of the anger and negative emotions that you feel toward that person to flow into that sheet of paper. Make sure that you feel all of your negative emotions toward them; this is very important if you really want to get revenge.

5. Now lay the paper down and place the chicken heart on the person's name. Take one of your candles and drip enough wax onto the heart until it is almost covered. Do this as you visualize this person's face and feel all of the negative emotions that you have for them. Take your time until you're sure that all of your negative emotions have been transferred to the paper.

6. Carefully fold the paper, securing it with twine to make sure that it holds the heart. Leave the package inside of the circle until all the candles have gone out.

7. Once they've gone out, bury the entire package under a big tree. Leave and don't look back. Never go back to that heart again.

Simple Journey Jinx

Have you ever had someone in your life who seems intent on ruining every day of your life while at the same time seems to live on cloud nine? They're always going on vacation and enjoying themselves while making your life miserable? Why not make their next trip just as miserable as they have been making your life?

WHEN TO PERFORM THE SPELL

On a Tuesday or during a First Quarter moon

HOW LONG IT TAKES

10 minutes

WHAT YOU'LL NEED

- A piece of paper
- The person's name
- A glass of ice water
- Salt

STEPS

1. Write the person's name on the piece of paper.
2. Sprinkle the salt into the water, then place the paper into the water. As you watch the paper soak, repeat this spell:

You wouldn't leave me alone

Causing me to want to flip.
Now you are going on a trip
But during your stay
It's going to rain every single day.

Siphoning Happiness Spell

This spell is going to take a bit more magic because it is a long-lasting spell that completely drains someone's happiness from their lives. You can use this spell on anyone, but it works best on a person who has tried to take or has successfully taken your happiness from you.

WHEN TO PERFORM THE SPELL

On a Monday or during a Waxing Crescent moon

HOW LONG IT TAKES

20 minutes

WHAT YOU'LL NEED

- Two pieces of paper
- Latex gloves
- A pen
- Basil – to siphon up the happiness
- A ribbon

STEPS

1. Write your name and the other person's name on the two sheets of paper.
2. Place the gloves side by side with the palms facing up. Place the two sheets of paper on the gloves, one on each glove. Place the basil (which represents happiness) on the other person's name.

3. Leave it there for 10 seconds, and then move the basil to your glove.

4. Remove the paper with the other person's name from their glove, placing that glove on top of the basil and binding everything together with the ribbon, making sure that your piece of paper and the basil remain between the gloves. Then say:

You left me empty-handed
You were rude and unkind
The next time you want something
You will be denied
As my prospects rise
Yours will fall
As my happiness increases
Yours will disappear

∼

More and More and More Curse

This spell curses the target with unwanted weight gain, which can be extra painful for the vain. The person will continue to gain weight, no matter how hard they try to stop. The only way for them to stop gaining weight is for you to break the spell and dispose of the remnants.

WHEN TO PERFORM THE SPELL

On a Friday or during a First Quarter moon

HOW LONG IT TAKES

20 minutes

WHAT YOU'LL NEED

- One banana
- One strawberry
- Two cups of saltwater
- Two avocados
- A blender
- One glass baking dish
- A freezer
- A picture of the person

STEPS

1. Blend the banana, strawberry, and avocado separately before casting your circle for this spell.

2. Once you have cast your circle, place the banana and the strawberry in the baking dish. For the next five minutes, you will meditate, focusing on the person you want to gain weight. You will visualize them gaining the amount of weight that you want them to gain.

3. After meditating, you will add the avocado to the pan and say this three times:

Add more to whom I desire.

4. Pour the saltwater into the glass pan. Meditate on the photograph for another two minutes, imagining what they would look like with the extra weight.

5. After the two minutes are up, place their picture in the pan. Close the circle.

Place the pan in your freezer and keep it there until the effects that you desire are achieved. Once the effects have been achieved, you can dispose of the remains of the spell.

∼

Humiliation Hex

Have you ever had someone humiliate you in public? It is something that sticks with you for a long time. You may never really get over it. The good news is that there is a very simple spell that will help you get your revenge.

WHEN TO PERFORM THE SPELL

On a Tuesday or during a Last Quarter moon

HOW LONG IT TAKES

5 minutes

WHAT YOU'LL NEED

- Paper
- A pen
- A freezer

STEPS

1. Write down why you want to humiliate the person on the piece of paper. It could be something they said or something that they did to you.
2. Place the paper deep in your freezer where no one will find it and say:

A good friend I could have been

But you are filled with dysfunction
Next time you are out in public
You will suffer an embarrassing wardrobe malfunction.

Tossing and Turning Curse

The feather of a raven is the secret ingredient to this spell, and while you may have to endure a bit of a stench, you will rest easy knowing that they are not.

WHEN TO PERFORM THE SPELL

At night, on a Tuesday or during a Last Quarter moon

HOW LONG IT TAKES

20 minutes

WHAT YOU'LL NEED

- The feather of a raven
- A tapered black candle
- Dirt from a graveyard
- A shallow dish

STEPS

1. Begin by carving the name of your target into the candle.
2. Place the dirt from the graveyard into the dish and stand the candle in the dirt.
3. Light the candle and say:

The power of the black raven
That flies above our head
The power of the black feather

The power from the smoke as well as the dead

4. Place the feather in the candle flame and light it.
5. This is going to smell really bad. Hold on to the feather as long as you can but don't burn your fingers.
Call out the person's name and say:

Restful sleep will not be yours!

6. Quickly blow out the candle.

Leave the candle where it sits until the next night at midnight. You will then snap the candle in half and stick both halves into the grave-yard dirt and leave it.

Pied Piper Curse

Rats, mice, fleas, spiders, snakes, and all other creatures that strike fear into the mind of the person you want revenge against will infest their home if you use this spell.

WHEN TO PERFORM THE SPELL

At night, on a Tuesday or during a Last Quarter moon

HOW LONG IT TAKES

1 hour

WHAT YOU'LL NEED

- Pictures of different vermin. You can get these from nature magazines, or you can print them off the internet
- A sheet of paper
- A pen
- The address of the person to whom you want to send the vermin
- Seeds, nuts, and other items that these creatures eat
- A white candle
- A piece of white material
- Twine

STEPS

1. Begin by laying the white piece of material out flat. You will

do all of your work on this because in the end, everything is wrapped in this material.

2. Place on the white material the pictures of the vermin with which you want to infest this person's house.

3. Write the person's address on the piece of paper and place it on the material as well.

4. Sprinkle the seeds, nuts, and other food over the pictures.

5. Place the candle in the middle of all of the pictures and recite:

Annoying you are and annoyed you will be
Creatures will come, but none you will see
Chewing and gnawing
Creeping and digging
As hard as you try
You won't catch any

6. Light the candle and allow it to burn until it goes out on its own.

Once the candle goes out, wrap everything together in the material and tie the bundle with the twine. Bury this as close as you possibly can to the person's house. Burying it in their yard is going to make this spell work best.

Chaotic Wind Curse

If you really want to cause a lot of damage to a person, this is the spell for you. It blows chaos into their life. It can manifest is strange ways, but chaos in any part of their life will tend to spread to other areas.

WHEN TO PERFORM THE SPELL

On a Wednesday or during a Waxing Crescent moon

HOW LONG IT TAKES

20 minutes

WHAT YOU'LL NEED

- A black candle
- Red pepper flakes
- A white piece of material
- A black marker
- A picture of the person

STEPS

1. On the white piece of material, draw eight arrows in a radial pattern to represent chaos.
2. Place your candle in the center of this pattern. Sprinkle the red pepper flakes around the candle.
3. Place the person's picture under the candle and say:

No longer will you have peace,

Chaos will rule your home
Even when your tears fall
Chaos will continue to roam.

4. Light the candle and allow it to burn until it burns out on its own.

~

Jalopy Jinx

I absolutely love using this spell on mechanics who think they can overcharge me or who don't want to do the work but want to get paid. I also hate when a mechanic tells me that there is something wrong with my car when clearly there is not. This little revenge spell comes in handy in those situations. It is also great to use on those who like to double-park, like to bang their doors into your car, cut you off in traffic, or just annoy you in life.

WHEN TO PERFORM THE SPELL

On a Wednesday or during a Last Quarter moon

HOW LONG IT TAKES

10 minutes

WHAT YOU'LL NEED

- A sheet of paper
- A pen
- The person's license plate number
- The make and model of the car
- A bit of cayenne pepper
- A small paper bag

STEPS

1. Write the person's license plate number as well as the make and the model of the car on the sheet of paper.

2. Place the paper into the bag, and sprinkle in the cayenne pepper.

3. Fold the bag closed, and shake it as you recite:

Trouble will come to your car
As you brought trouble to me
It will not start, it will not go
A piece of junk it will be.

~

11

LOVE AND WAR

Some witches consider love spells, or spells for seduction, to be wicked, because it controls someone else's mind. But none of these spells can turn a person into a mindless zombie. You can only fan the flames of love where there was interest already.

As to war, well, in my experience, you can never hate someone as much as you can hate someone you once loved. All that emotion makes for some powerful spells in this chapter, but be sure to approach each spell with a clear intent. Raging emotions are powerful, but lack focus.

Seduction Spell

Seduction spells take a lot of work, because you are working on another person, and they are usually long-term spells. This spell, while it does not call for a lot of ingredients, does have to be done over a period of time. You may have to cast the spell more than once, but I assure you it will work.

WHEN TO PERFORM THE SPELL

On a Tuesday or during a Waxing Crescent moon

HOW LONG IT TAKES

10 minutes a day for nine consecutive days

WHAT YOU'LL NEED

- A piece of attractive paper
- A pen
- A red candle
- A heat-proof dish

STEPS

1. Write your name on the paper and the other person's name under yours. Make sure that you write your name on top because that means you will be the dominant person. Under your names, write down the other person's birthdate and then your own birthdate.

2. Draw a heart around this information and carefully trace over it all three times.

3. Fold the paper as small as you can and light it with the candle, dropping it onto the heat-proof dish and allowing it to burn to ash. While the paper is burning, repeat this three times:

Light of the flame,
Bright as fire
Red is the color of our desire.

4. Continue this process every night for nine days in a row.

You may decide that you want to save the ashes in a small box until you are finished with the spell and want to release them into the wind.

Siren's Call Spell

Let me be clear, you can't force someone to fall in love with you if they just are not interested. All love spells, even this one, require at least a degree of interest from the other person, and the more interested they are before the spell, the better. Love spells fan the ember of desire into a flame. They also require more work than a revenge spell.

WHEN TO PERFORM THE SPELL

On a Monday or during a First Quarter moon

HOW LONG IT TAKES

10 minutes a day for nine consecutive days

WHAT YOU'LL NEED

- Red ribbon
- Two small pieces of parchment paper
- Wooden matches
- A wooden pencil
- One large piece of parchment paper
- One pink candle
- Cinnamon incense – to increase desire
- Emerald – to bring loyalty
- Sandalwood oil – to make wishes come true
- Jade – to manifest dreams
- Rose quartz – to turn negative energy into positive energy

STEPS

1. Anoint your pink candle with a few drops of sandalwood oil.

2. Light your incense and the candle.

3. Using the wooden pencil, write your name on one of the small pieces of parchment paper and the name of the object of your love on the other. Draw a heart around both names.

4. Take your candle and drip a bit of wax onto each of the hearts. While you are dripping the wax onto the hearts, visualize what you want to happen.

5. Use your large piece of paper to write down what you want to happen. Do not rush the process. When you are done, fold the two small pieces of paper together with the large piece.

6. Tie the papers together with the red ribbon, making three knots.

7. Place the emerald, jade, and quartz on the top of the paper to charge it.

Let everything sit until your candle burns out, then take your paper package, leaving the crystals behind, and hide it in your bedroom. Make sure that no one else will be able to find it.

Domination Oil

Sometimes you need to control your partner, and this oil will help you gain the upper hand right when you need it. This will not give you the power to control your partner's mind. But your partner will agree with you more often and will be more likely to see things from your point of view.

This is actually an oil infused with magic, which you'll use by applying to your partner. There is no chanting to be done, only mixing. Once the mixing is done, there is waiting.

WHEN TO PERFORM THE SPELL

You should start preparing the oil on a Friday or during a First Quarter moon

HOW LONG IT TAKES

10 minutes to prepare, then one month to infuse the oil

WHAT YOU'LL NEED

- A jar
- A red cloth
- Three coffee beans – to stimulate
- One teaspoon of powdered orris root – to draw love
- Dried calamus root – for control
- Dried licorice root – for domination
- Sunflower oil – for loyalty
- The peel of a green clementine, dried – for attraction

STEPS

1. Place all of the ingredients except for the red cloth into the jar.
2. Place the red cloth over the jar and allow the oil to infuse for one month.

Place this oil in areas that you know your partner will touch. You can also transfer the oil to your partner by touching them while it is on your hands. Your partner will have to keep their agreements with you, or they will suffer greatly. You will quickly become the dominant person in the relationship because they will suffer when they do not do as you want them to.

Three's a Crowd Vinegar Jar

Vinegar jars are used to banish someone from your life. This spell does not cause anything to happen to the target except for them to leave you alone and butt out of your life.

Because this spell uses running water, there is no reversing it, so make sure that when you cast it, you are truly done with the person, and there is no chance for reconciliation.

WHEN TO PERFORM THE SPELL

On a Saturday or during a Full Moon

HOW LONG IT TAKES

20 minutes, then a 3 day wait

WHAT YOU'LL NEED

- A black candle
- A picture of the person or a piece of paper with their name written on it
- A jar
- Running water, like a river or stream
- Vinegar – to drive someone away
- Salt – to purify

STEPS

1. Begin by lighting your black candle and saying:

Leave me this day
Your evil is no longer welcome; you may not stay
You do not belong
Your presence is wrong
It's time to go away
Leave me this day.

2. Place their picture in the jar and fill it up with vinegar.
3. Toss one pinch of salt into the jar.
4. Place the lid on the jar.
5. Allow the candle to burn out on its own. Let the picture soak in the jar for three days while sitting in the sun.
6. On the third day, take the jar to the water source and pour the vinegar into the water while saying:

Now it is time for you to go
Where you will be, I do not want to know.

The person will no longer bother you or interject themselves into your life.

∾

Sour Break Up Spell

Using a lemon to break up a relationship is an ancient magical practice. This spell takes that to the next level by adding in the hair of a cat and a dog - to make them fight like cats and dogs.

WHEN TO PERFORM THE SPELL

On a Monday or during a Waning Gibbous

HOW LONG IT TAKES

30 minutes

WHAT YOU'LL NEED

- Piece of paper
- A black dog hair
- A black cat hair
- Black pepper – to irritate
- A lemon – to sour
- Vinegar – to drive people apart
- Black wax
- A pen
- Scissors
- A rusty nail
- Black thread

STEPS

1. Write the names of both people on the piece of paper. Do not write them large; make sure they're not bigger than the center of the lemon.

2. Cut the names apart and put a bit of vinegar on each of the names.

3. Cut your lemon in half. Make sure the names are facing each other and place them on either side of the inside of the lemon.

4. Place the black dog hair on one name and the black cat hair on the other. Sprinkle pepper on both.

5. Carefully bring the two lemon halves together, sandwiching everything in between. Seal it up with the black wax and drive the rusty nail through both halves.

6. Tie the lemon together with the black thread.

Once your lemon is prepared, you will bury it where the couple lives.

The Relationship Flush

If the last breakup spell wasn't strong enough, this one will be, but it comes at the price of another nasty ingredient – your own urine. You'll also need to work with live animals, but don't worry, they won't be harmed.

The incantation in this spells assumes a man and a woman in the relationship, but it works just as well on same sex couples.

WHEN TO PERFORM THE SPELL

On a Monday or during a Waning Gibbous moon

HOW LONG IT TAKES

30 minutes

WHAT YOU'LL NEED

- A pot
- An egg from a black chicken
- A dog
- A cat
- Your urine
- Gloves

STEPS

1. Boil the egg from the black chicken in your own urine. Yep, you read that right. You might want to make sure that you don't use one of your favorite cooking pots for this recipe.

2. Once the egg has boiled, peel it. (This is where the gloves come in.) You might also want to throw the pot away at this point.

3. Cut the egg in half.

4. Feed one half of the egg to the black dog and say:

Just like dogs hate cats, (the man's name) will also hate (the woman's name).

5. Feed the other half of the egg to the black cat and say:

Just like cats hate dogs, (the woman's name) will also hate (the man's name).

∾

Forever Hold Your Peace Curse

If it is out of spite, revenge, or because you want one of the participants for yourself, you don't have to watch anyone walk down the aisle if you don't want to. Be prepared, though; this spell is going to take some serious mental strength and a lot of work.

WHEN TO PERFORM THE SPELL

On a Monday or during a Waning Gibbous moon

HOW LONG IT TAKES

1 hour

WHAT YOU'LL NEED

- Four black candles
- Paper
- Sea salt
- Fireproof dish
- Rainwater
- Charcoal
- Dirt
- Shovel
- Matches
- A pouch
- Ginger oil – to energize the spell
- Lavender incense – to remove the couple's luck
- Basil – to soak up the couple's happiness
- Salt – to banish the couple from each other

- Cayenne pepper – to irritate

STEPS

1. Cast your circle with the sea salt. It is important that your circle is big enough for you to stand in while you are performing the ritual.

2. Anoint each of your candles with the ginger oil and place one candle in each direction, north, south, east, and west.

3. Place your fireproof dish goes in the center of the circle.

4. Light your candles and the lavender incense.

5. Now use the charcoal to write on the piece of paper the name of the couple whose marriage you want to stop.

6. Once the names are written down, take the ginger oil and sprinkle it over them.

7. Tear the paper into three and place it on your fireproof dish. Sprinkle the salt, basil, and cayenne pepper over the paper.

8. Pick up the candle that represents the west and drip some of the wax on top of the paper, saying,

By the powers of the west, fulfill my request.

9. Pick up the candle representing the south, saying,

By the powers of the south, stop the love in their mouth.

10. Pick up the candle representing the east, saying,

By the powers of the east, stop the marriage, the love has deceased.

11. With the candle representing the north, say,

By the powers of the north, bring my plea forth.

As you say this, you should visualize the relationship coming to an end and the wedding being called off. You will need to be in a deep meditative state. Once this is accomplished, you will burn everything in the fireproof dish. Add in a bit of rainwater and dirt. Mix it all well and place it in a pouch.

Let your candles burn out on their own, and then bury your pouch somewhere shady near a tree.

The Home Wrecker Jar

Causing the end of a marriage is something that you should not take lightly. It is also something that takes a lot of magic and a lot of work.

These two people have taken vows and have become one, so separating them is a difficult task. However, it can be done. It is important to know that these types of spells only work if one of the people in the marriage no longer wants to be part of the marriage or the vows have been broken.

WHEN TO PERFORM THE SPELL

On a Monday or during a First Quarter moon

HOW LONG IT TAKES

1 hour

WHAT YOU'LL NEED

- A jar with a lid
- A knife to carve with
- A tablespoon of olive oil
- A handful of soil from a place where nothing will grow
- Sheet of paper
- A pencil without an eraser
- 13 needles
- 13 nails
- Seven pieces of broken glass
- Seven black candles
- Two black strings

- Two tablespoons of red pepper flakes – to irritate
- One tablespoon of black pepper – to prevent the couple from reconciling
- Two tablespoons of cayenne pepper – to energize the spell
- One tablespoon of poppyseeds – to cause confusion and distrust
- Two tablespoons of mustard seed – to drive them apart
- A tablespoon of vinegar – to sour the relationship

STEPS

1. Carve the first names of the married couple into all seven candles.
2. Mix the oil and the vinegar together and use it to anoint the candles.
3. Place the black candles around your circle and light them.
4. Write the names of the couple on the paper, one on top of the other. Turn the paper over and write down what you want to happen to them, for example, DIVORCE. You can be more specific if you want.
5. Tear the paper, separating their names. Roll up each of the papers and tie them with the string. Place the rolled papers in the jar.
6. Add the 13 nails and the 13 needles to the jar and say,

Needles and nails are painful reminders that your relationship is over.

7. The broken glass goes in next. Say,

Broken glass, just like the broken relationship, broken bond, and broken vows.

8. Add in the red, black, and cayenne pepper to the jar and say:

Heated emotions will bring fights, arguments, and discord to your relationship.

9. Add the poppy seeds to the jar and say:

Hate, anger, and miscommunication fill your relationship.

10. Add the mustard seeds to the jar, and say:

These represent the negative feelings that you have for one another.

11. Add the dirt to the jar and say:

This is infertile soil where nothing can grow, just as no love can ever grow between the two of you.

12. Add in the vinegar to the jar and say:

Your relationship is sour, and all of the negative feelings that you have for each other are forever preserved.

13. Place the lid on the jar and close it tightly. Shake it well and focus on what you want to happen to the couple.

14. Sprinkle some cayenne pepper on one of the black candles and drip some of the wax on the lid of the jar. Stick the candle to the jar and allow all of the candles to burn out.

Bury the jar near where they live. Ending a marriage will take time, and the stronger their relationship, the longer it will take.

Forever Alone Jar

You can use this spell to keep someone single, which may be a benefit for the rest of humanity.

WHEN TO PERFORM THE SPELL

On a Friday or during a Dark moon

HOW LONG IT TAKES

10 minutes, then a few moments every day for 60 days

WHAT YOU'LL NEED

- A glass jar
- A picture of the person
- Apple cider vinegar – to make the person sour
- Garlic – to keep people away
- Sage – to remove the person's wisdom
- Mint – to purify the person (from other people)
- Thyme – to remove the person's luck
- Lavender – to remove the energy of love from a person

STEPS

1. Place the picture in the jar and sprinkle all of the herbs over it.
2. Pour the apple cider vinegar into the jar on top of the herbs and picture.

3. Place the lid on the jar, and every day for the next 60 days, shake the mixture carefully. Say this:

Love is not for you
You proved you can't be true
Happiness you don't deserve
Loneliness you will serve

After 60 days, leave the jar in a dark place for as long as you want the spell to last.

Impotence Hex

Has the man in your life been unfaithful and hurt you deeply? Maybe you want to take revenge by making him impotent? If so, then this is the perfect spell. This spell is not only going to make a man lose his sex drive, but he will also suffer from erectile dysfunction when he tries to have sex.

WHEN TO PERFORM THE SPELL

On a Wednesday or during a Last Quarter moon

HOW LONG IT TAKES

30 minutes

WHAT YOU'LL NEED

- One white candle
- Three black candles
- 10 grains of rice in a bowl
- A picture of the person
- Two amethysts – to absorb the peace in his life
- Three cloves of garlic – to drive people away
- Myrrh incense – to remove sensual feelings
- Ginseng root – to remove passion from the man

STEPS

1. Place your white candle in the north position, and black candles in the south, east, and west.

2. Light your incense before placing all of your garlic cloves, amethyst, and rice in your bowl. Place the bowl to the right of your north candle and your incense to the left.

3. Place the picture of the person in front of the north candle.

4. Take the impotence filter and place it next to the incense.

5. Light the other candles.

6. Pour a few drops of the candle wax from the candle representing the north onto the picture.

7. Return the candle to its position at the north.

8. Pick up the bowl with one hand and the ginseng root with the other as you focus on the picture. Say this:

Nemesis, Goddess of Impotence, by this spell make (the person's name) impotent very soon and forever.

9. Put the black candles out one by one before putting out the white candle. After you put out the candles, exit the circle and allow the incense to burn.

Binding Love Spell

When you have been with one person for a long time, it can be very tempting to see what someone else has to offer. If you are afraid that your partner is going to cheat on you or that they have already cheated on you, casting a spell will ensure their faithfulness in the future. This spell will ensure that they are no longer tempted to cheat on you and have no desire for anyone but you.

WHEN TO PERFORM THE SPELL

On a Tuesday or during a Full moon

HOW LONG IT TAKES

1 hour

WHAT YOU'LL NEED

- Brown cloth cut into large pieces
- A pink candle
- A needle
- One of your partner's personal items that they have touched
- Four pinches of sand
- Musk incense
- Cherry oil – for control in romance

STEPS

1. Use your large pieces of brown cloth to cover all of the mirrors in the room. You should also make sure that every window in the room has been closed.

2. Anoint your candle with the cherry oil. Using the needle, carve your partner's name into the candle and then anoint the candle with the cherry oil a second time. While anointing the candle the second time, focus intensely on your relationship with your partner and on the faithfulness that you want from them.

3. Light your musk incense and place it in a position so that the smoke will travel to the center of the circle.

4. Place your candle in the center of the circle, then place your partner's personal item in front of the candle.

5. Light the candle.

6. Kneel in front of the candle and meditate, focusing on your relationship and your partner being protected in every circumstance. The most effective way to make this spell work is to use your own words as you meditate. When you have finished, take a pinch of sand and throw it to the four corners (one to each corner).

7. Open the windows in the room and allow the candle and incense to burn out on their own.

You should be able to tell almost immediately if your spell has worked. If it has been successful, your partner will begin paying more attention to you and your relationship. Your partner's eyes will no longer wander.

Jealous Feelings Jinx

Jealousy is often used to cause relationships to end, but it can also be used to make a straying partner feel stronger emotions for the one they're supposed to be with. This is one of those spells where the outcome can be hard to predict, so be sure to use some form of divination and ask if you should proceed with it.

WHEN TO PERFORM THE SPELL

On a Sunday or during a First Quarter moon

HOW LONG IT TAKES

15 minutes

WHAT YOU'LL NEED

- A picture of the target
- A pocket mirror
- Red lipstick
- Tape

STEPS

1. Tape the picture of the person to the back of the mirror.
2. As you look in the mirror, apply the red lipstick as thickly as possible. Continue to look at yourself in the mirror and begin kissing the mirror as if you are the most amazing person in the world.
3. While you are kissing the mirror, imagine that you are

kissing someone other than the person in the picture.

Transmit the message to the person that you are amazing and that it is entirely possible for you to be kissing someone else.

The target will start to believe that there is something going on behind their back. Like I said though, it can be hard to predict how they'll react.

Banish Your Ex Hex

Sometimes when you end a relationship, your ex just won't let things go. This spell will put an end to that. It does need to be cast on a full moon at midnight, which can be inconvenient, but it will ensure that your ex leaves you alone for as long as you want them to.

WHEN TO PERFORM THE SPELL

On a Full moon at midnight

HOW LONG IT TAKES

15 minutes

WHAT YOU'LL NEED

- A piece of paper with your ex's name written on it
- A freezer
- A plastic freezer container
- Fish
- Water

STEPS

1. Crunch the paper with your ex's name written on it into a ball.
2. Place this ball of paper into your plastic container, along with the bit of fish.
3. Add in the water. Hold the container over your head and say:

By the power of the Moon
May this magic work fast
May he (or she) not be immune
Make him (or her) gone. Make it last.

4. Place the container in your freezer in an area where no one will disturb it or find it.

Leave it in the freezer for as long as you need to or until this ex is completely gone from your life. When you no longer need the spell, dispose of the remnants in running water as far away from your home as possible.

ALL THAT GLITTERS

One of the most satisfying ways to get revenge on a person is to hit them where it hurts the most - in their pocketbook. Most people can handle stress in any other area of their life, as long as their finances are okay, but when their finances take a hit, they tend to start freaking out. These spells are for those who have really done you wrong, because let's face it, they are the ones who really deserve to be punished.

Not only are we going to cover spells that you can cast to get revenge on others, but we will also go over a few that will help your own finances. Sometimes the best revenge is living well.

Money Draw Spell

A money draw spell may not seem evil, but as I've mentioned, that money has to come from someone else, and they may very well consider this spell wicked. Here we'll create Money Draw Oil, a magical oil whose properties cause money to flow to you. We'll then use it in a candle spell, so the fire of the candle can energize the oil and get things moving.

WHEN TO PERFORM THE SPELL

On a Sunday or during a Waxing Crescent moon

HOW LONG IT TAKES

10 minutes a day for seven days

WHAT YOU'LL NEED

- Three drops of cinnamon oil – to energize the spell and to attract your intentions
- Three drops of mint oil – to draw luck to you
- Three drops of basil oil – to draw money to you
- One white candle – to symbolize you
- One green candle – to symbolize money

STEPS

1. Mix all three oils together and anoint your candles with the mixture. As you anoint your candles, it is important to focus on your reason for casting the spell, as well as the money that you want to gain.

2. Once this is done, place the candles seven inches apart. Light both candles and say:

Money, money flow to me
In abundance as big as the sea
Like a river flowing free
As I speak it, let it be.

3. After one verse, move your white candle one inch closer to your green candle. Put the flame out but do not blow it out. You can use a candle snuffer or just wet your fingertips and use them.

Continue to do this for the next six days, moving the candles closer each day. On day seven, the candles will be touching, and your spell will be complete. Do not put the candles out on this day, but instead allow them to burn themselves out.

Luck Draw Spell

If you do not have much good luck, this spell can turn that around for you, just remember that good luck for you may be bad luck for someone else. If you are concerned that your good luck is wearing out, cast this spell to give it an extra boost.

WHEN TO PERFORM THE SPELL

On a Wednesday or during a First Quarter moon

HOW LONG IT TAKES

15 minutes

WHAT YOU'LL NEED

- A brand-new penny
- Heat-proof dish
- A blue candle
- A lighter or long matches
- Eucalyptus oil – to ward off bad luck
- A four-leaf clover – to draw good luck

STEPS

1. Anoint your blue candle with eucalyptus oil. Then light your candle and place it in the middle of your circle.
2. Flip your coin until it lands on heads three times in a row.
3. Place the four-leaf clover in your heat-proof dish and burn it, saying:

Lady Luck, I need your blessings
So, I give this offering to you
My luck will be impressing
As I speak it, you make it true.

Allow the candle to burn out on its own.

The Hot Hand Enchantment

Like the last spell, this one will draw luck to you, but this one focuses on luck at gambling. Don't expect it to win the lottery for you, but you can use it to get going with a hot streak at a card table. The goal of the spell is to enchant a poker chip, which you can carry with you when you need it.

WHEN TO PERFORM THE SPELL

On a Wednesday or during a First Quarter moon

HOW LONG IT TAKES

15 minutes

WHAT YOU'LL NEED

- One poker chip
- One white candle
- One gold marker
- Peridot crystal – to draw money to you
- Cinnamon oil – to energize the spell and draw luck

STEPS

1. Carve a sigil for good luck into your candle and anoint it with cinnamon oil. The sigil can be whatever you think looks lucky or like money - a "$" will do just fine.
2. Light the candle and use the gold marker to draw the same sigil on your poker chip.

3. Lay your peridot crystal on the chip and leave it until the candle burns out.

Whenever you gamble, you will carry both the poker chip and the crystal with you.

Gambler's Ruin Jinx

This is the exact opposite of the previous spell. How sweet it is to sit back and watch someone who was once cocky in their gambling lose everything they bet. A night that they thought would be full of joy as they took everyone else's money turns into a night of gloom and disappointment for them.

WHEN TO PERFORM THE SPELL

On a Wednesday or during a Last Quarter moon

HOW LONG IT TAKES

20 minutes

WHAT YOU'LL NEED

- A picture of the person
- A pair of dice
- Black pepper
- An outside location

STEPS

1. Dig a hole a few inches deep.
2. Place the dice in the hole, making sure that snake eyes are up.
3. Cover the dice with pepper and say:

Your luck is gone
Now in the hole

Terrible things are going to happen
This is the goal.

4. Focus on your target's picture and begin filling the hole with dirt.
5. When the hole is filled, stomp on it hard to make sure that it is completely packed down. Leave the area and allow the magic to do its work.

Debtor's Binding

Some people think paying debts is optional, even if it leaves the person they owe in financial difficulty. This spell turns up the heat on a person who owes you money until they pay you back.

WHEN TO PERFORM THE SPELL

On a Thursday or during a Waxing Crescent moon

HOW LONG IT TAKES

20 minutes

WHAT YOU'LL NEED

- A sheet of paper
- Two hot peppers
- A rubber band
- A pen

STEPS

1. On one side of the paper, write the person's name who owes you. On the other side, write:

As the paper grows hot, so shall you, until you pay me what you owe.

2. Fold the paper to about the same size as the pepper, ensuring that the person's name is on the outside.

3. Place the paper between the two peppers and use the rubber band to secure it all together. Leave it in a safe place.

The person will bring you what they owe you within a few days because they will not be able to stand the heat.

Jubilee Spell

Hundreds of years ago, the Pope would occasionally call for a year of Jubilee, in which all debts were forgiven. We all make mistakes in life, and many of us end up getting ourselves into debt that we can't pay or that could take us the rest of our lives to pay. It happens. The good news is that there is a spell that can banish that debt from your life. Magically, money will be found to pay off your debt, or the debtor will simply decide that you no longer owe it. It is amazing how things work out.

WHEN TO PERFORM THE SPELL

On a Sunday or during a Waxing Gibbous moon

HOW LONG IT TAKES

30 minutes

WHAT YOU'LL NEED

- A purple candle
- Parchment paper
- An envelope
- A pen
- Bayberry oil – to draw money
- Lavender incense – to bring general good luck
- Chamomile flowers – to bring luck in money
- Salt – to banish the debt
- Running water, such as a stream or river

STEPS

1. Anoint your candle with the lavender oil and light it.

2. Write down all of your debts on the parchment paper.

3. Look into the flame of the candle as you think about your debt. Begin to imagine what your life would be like if you were finally out of debt.

4. Look back at your list and sprinkle it with a bit of salt.

5. Fold the paper so that it will fit into your envelope. Place it into the envelope and seal it.

6. On the envelope, write,

Debt-free I want to be
Whatever it takes, come set me free
As I will it, let it be.

7. Place a bit of the bayberry oil on the corners of the envelope and then pass the envelope through the incense smoke seven times. Do the same thing over the flame of the candle.

8. Allow the candle to burn out completely. If your envelope catches fire, don't worry, just put it out.

Finally, bring your envelope and your flowers to a stream or river, placing both in the water together. Make it very clear to yourself that you will never allow yourself to get in debt ever again.

~

Business Butcher Curse

Sometimes you want to make a person suffer slowly as they watch their business fall apart. The best way to do that is to make their customers disappear. After all, customers are what keep a business alive. As soon as sales are affected, the business begins to hurt.

This is another one of those special spells that uses some unsavory items that could make you a little uncomfortable at first, but let's remember that we use these items because they are so powerful. In this case we'll use a cow's liver. In ancient Rome they used animal livers for divination. The look of the liver could tell the future. In the same way, you can use a liver to *create* the future.

WHEN TO PERFORM THE SPELL

During a Dark moon

HOW LONG IT TAKES

About one hour spread out over several days

WHAT YOU'LL NEED

- A black cloth
- A needle
- A cow's liver
- Plain white paper
- A red marker
- A metal container
- Rue leaves – to cleanse the store of customers

STEPS

1. Wrap your cow liver in the black cloth and let it sit overnight in the metal container. Squeeze the liver while it is wrapped in the cloth to ensure that the cloth is fully soaked in the cow's blood. This act will squeeze the metaphorical life's blood out of the store.

2. On the following day, unwrap the liver and soak the cloth with the blood before spreading it on the table.

3. Place five of the rue leaves on the center of the cloth.

4. Using the red marker, write the name of the business on the plain white paper. Wrap it all up and place the cloth in an area where no one will find it or look at it for two nights.

5. On the second night, take it out and prick your finger with the needle, dripping three drops of your blood onto the package. Think about what you want to happen to the business. In this case, you want them to lose customers. Perhaps there is more to it than that, though. Maybe you want their customers to instead come to your family's store.

Once you have finished, light on fire everything in the metal container. You may need to add some kerosene or lighter fluid to get it going. As you watch it all burn, imagine the customers walking out on the business.

Going Out of Business Hex

If watching customers slowly leave a business is not the type of revenge that works for you, maybe completely ruining a business is something that appeals more to your taste. This spell is fairly easy and does not require as much magic as the previous spell; however, it can bring a business to its knees.

Part of this work involves creating Cursing Oil, which should be part of every wicked witch's pantry. It's called for again in the next several spell.

WHEN TO PERFORM THE SPELL

During a Dark moon

HOW LONG IT TAKES

As long as it takes for the candle to burn down

WHAT YOU'LL NEED

- A picture of the business
- A small black candle
- A sachet
- A heat-proof dish
- A lighter or wooden matches
- A black marker
- The Cursing Oil. Equal parts of:
- Poke root – call evil spirits to the business
- Graveyard dirt – the cause the business to die

- Poppy seeds – to cause confusion
- Red pepper – to cause irritation
- Vinegar – to sour customers
- Black pepper – to cause pain
- Mullein leaf – for control

STEPS

1. Mix all of the herbs together and put them in a jar. Fill the jar with olive oil as a carrier oil and stir. You've just created the Cursing Oil.

2. Anoint your candle with a few drops of the Cursing Oil.

3. Write words like "Out of business", "Bankrupt", and "Ruined" all over the front of the picture of the business using the black marker.

4. On the back of the picture write:

Your business is gone
What you worked for is in shambles
You proved to be a con
While everyone watches you scramble.

5. Place the picture face down under the candle and light the candle.

6. Just before the candle burns itself out, take the picture out from under it and burn it in your heat-proof dish. Place the ashes in the sachet.

7. Go to the business and allow the ashes to scatter into the air. Say:

Like the ashes, so will you drift away.

Empty Wallet Curse

Causing a person financial difficulty is one of the best ways to get revenge. Hitting someone's finances can completely destroy their life, and if they have caused enough damage in yours, maybe that is exactly what they deserve. It is very important to follow the directions precisely, because you do not want it to backfire on you.

WHEN TO PERFORM THE SPELL

On a Tuesday or during

HOW LONG IT TAKES

As long as it takes for the candle to burn down

WHAT YOU'LL NEED

- One black candle
- The Cursing Oil that you made for the last spell to ruin a business
- A needle
- A picture of your target
- A heat-proof dish

STEPS

1. Carve a dollar sign into your candle and with a needle put a slash mark through it, canceling it out.
2. Anoint your candle with your Cursing Oil and place your target's picture underneath it.
3. Light the candle and say:

Money has been yours from the start
But now you will lose it all
The love of it you had in your heart
Now we will all see you fall.

4. Take the picture out from under the candle. Light it using the flame of the candle and let it burn in the heat-proof dish.
5. Allow the candle to burn out.

Remember, do not dispose of the remnants until you are finished with the spell, so put these ashes and the bit of the candle left in a safe place until you are ready to cancel out the spell and dispose of them.

Freezing Finances Binding

If you really want to go all out, you can cause a person to be completely financially ruined. This spell slowly causes their sources of income to dry up and their debts to mount, until they can't find a way out.

WHEN TO PERFORM THE SPELL

On a Sunday or during a Waning Gibbous moon

HOW LONG IT TAKES

As long as it takes for the candle to burn down

WHAT YOU'LL NEED

- A black candle
- Three pennies
- A cup
- Water
- A freezer
- A picture of the person
- A black marker
- Cursing Oil

STEPS

1. Anoint your black candle and the coins with the Cursing Oil.

2. Light your candle.

3. Place your coins in the cup.

4. Write BANKRUPT diagonally across the picture of the target and place the picture in the cup.

5. Pour the water into the cup, and say:

Bankrupt you will now be
Debt will take over thee
Money will slip through your hands
This curse you will not be able to withstand.

6. Place the cup in the freezer and allow the spell to work. Let the candle burn out on its own.

13

TRUE FRIENDS STAB YOU IN THE FRONT

S ometimes it is the people who are closest to you that you have to watch the most. These spells are for those of you who want to punish people who have done you wrong in your day-to-day life. Perhaps you have a "friend" who you think is lying to you or who is gossiping about you. Maybe a neighbor is driving you crazy, and you want to make them move, or perhaps you just want that one family member to stop interfering in your life.

Not every revenge spell has to be a painful curse. Some can simply put an end to behaviors that annoy us. They can make our lives easier and allow us to have the peace that we so deeply crave.

Liar's Lamentation

Finding out someone is spreading lies about you can be especially painful because it's so difficult to prove the truth, and so hard to accept that others would believe the lies in the first place. The first step to take to repair your reputation is to expose the liar.

WHEN TO PERFORM THE SPELL

On a Tuesday or during a Full moon

HOW LONG IT TAKES

30 minutes

WHAT YOU'LL NEED

- One onion
- A knife
- A small offering, such as a bit of wine or juice
- A place in nature

STEPS

1. Carve the person's name into the onion.
2. Carefully make a cut into the onion and begin peeling away the layers. As you peel each layer, imagine that you are tearing away the fronts that the person is putting up until the truth is exposed.
3. Take all of the pieces of the onion and toss them into a place

in nature where they will rot. As they rot, so will the person's deception and lies.

Leave your small offering for the nature spirits of the area, to assist you in your spell. As the onion rots over the next few days, you'll see the people around the person start to realize the truth of the situation, like a veil has been lifted from their eyes.

Loose Lips Binding

If you find out that someone is spreading gossip or rumors about you, this one is a good way to make them stop. You'll need to pay another trip to a butcher's shop, or at least a specialty food store, to get the cow's tongue the spell calls for.

WHEN TO PERFORM THE SPELL

On a Saturday or during a Dark moon

HOW LONG IT TAKES

30 minutes

WHAT YOU'LL NEED

- A cow's tongue
- A sheet of paper
- A knife
- A large nail
- A length of twine
- A pen

STEPS

1. Take the knife and slice down the center of the cow's tongue.
2. Write your target's name on the paper and slip it into the tongue where you made the slice.
3. Take the twine and wrap it around the tongue, binding it

tightly, ensuring that the cut is closed, and tie the twine together in a knot. Say this:

I'm out of your sight, I'm out of your mind
(the person's name) your wicked tongue I bind
Keep your words away from me
As I speak it, so will it be.

4. Pierce the tongue with the nail to really drive the point home.
5. Bury the remains far away from your house.

Banishing Jar

Sometimes you just need someone to go away – preferably far, far away. You can use this spell on anyone, from a former friend, an ex-lover, or a coworker you can't stand.

WHEN TO PERFORM THE SPELL

On a Tuesday or during a Waning Gibbous moon

HOW LONG IT TAKES

1 hour

WHAT YOU'LL NEED

- A small piece of paper
- A pen
- Glass jar with lid
- Vinegar
- Sea salt

STEPS

1. Write your target's name on the small piece of paper.
2. Fold the paper in half two times and think about the person leaving your life forever.
3. Place the paper in the jar.
4. Sprinkle the salt on the paper, making sure to completely cover the paper. As you do this, continue to think about the person leaving your life for good.

5. Next, add in about a capful of vinegar and say:

Leave my life, stay away from me
From you, I will finally be free
Go away; you are banished from here
You must go far. I don't want you near.

6. Place the lid on the jar and bury it as far away from your home as you can. Some witches throw the jar away, but as we talked about earlier in this book, I do not suggest doing that. Throwing the jar away will not complete the spell, and you will likely continue to have problems with this person.

You Are Not Wanted Here Hex

The effect of this spell is similar to the last one, but is intended for someone who lives in the same place as you. That means you'll know where they'll walk, so you can use foot track magic to affect them. Foot track magic comes from Hoodoo, and works by putting something in the path they'll walk through, which triggers the spell.

The spell takes a while to complete, because you're capturing the essence of the disappearing moon, and transferring that to the person you want to disappear.

WHEN TO PERFORM THE SPELL

Start on a Full moon and finish it on the Dark moon

HOW LONG IT TAKES

14 days

WHAT YOU'LL NEED

- A black candle
- A small piece of paper
- A pen or marker
- Something to carve with
- Vinegar – to sour the person's situation
- Poppy seeds – to cause confusion
- Red pepper flakes – to irritate the person and make them want to leave

STEPS

1. Grind up the poppy seeds and mix with the red pepper.
2. On the night of a Full moon, write the target's name on the small piece of paper. Follow this by saying:

Leave my home and do not return.

3. Put one drop of vinegar on the paper and roll it up.
4. Carve a hole in the candle large enough to fit the paper. If you are having a hard time carving into the candle, you can heat your carving tool.
5. Sprinkle the poppy seed and red pepper mixture onto the candle.
6. After the paper is inside the candle, light the candle and allow it to burn for nine minutes for 14 nights.

On the 14th night, toss the remnants into flowing water, but save some candle drippings or some ash. You will sprinkle this into the path of the person you want to leave your home.

Interference Intercession Spell

Some people like to give advice even when it's not wanted, and some go even further and will try and outright interfere in our lives, because they think they know best. This seems to happen to me with family members more often than not.

This simple spell won't hurt them, but will get them to mind their own business.

WHEN TO PERFORM THE SPELL

On a Saturday or during a Last Quarter moon

HOW LONG IT TAKES

10 minutes

WHAT YOU'LL NEED

- A small piece of a paper
- A gallon-sized freezer storage bag with zipper closure
- Three quarts of water
- A pen

STEPS

1. Write your target's name on the small piece of paper.
2. Place the paper in the bag and pour the three quarts of water into it.
3. Close the bag and place it in the freezer. Make sure it's somewhere no one will bother it or find it.

Once the bag is frozen, the person will be frozen from interfering in your life.

Move Away Curse

I created this spell when I had neighbors move in that pushed me to my limits and tested my patience. I was at my wit's end, and I figured I needed to find a way to solve the problem without risking jail time.

This spell calls for moon water, which is just water that's been left outside in the moonlight overnight. If possible, charge this moon water with the light of a Wanning Gibbous moon, because it's good for banishing things from your life. It also requires another nasty ingredient, as you'll see, but nasty ingredients are needed to power a spell to convince someone to leave the place they live.

WHEN TO PERFORM THE SPELL

On a Dark moon night

HOW LONG IT TAKES

1 hour

WHAT YOU'LL NEED

- A pint jar
- A pot
- One pint of moon water
- One pint of your urine
- The silver filings of a silver spoon or silver dime
- Three black peppercorns
- Two tablespoons of salt
- Three teaspoons of garlic powder

STEPS

1. Place all of these ingredients in a pan on the stove. Reduce everything down to one pint and pour it in a jar.
2. On the night of the Dark moon, sprinkle this on the neighbor's doorstep, and it will cause them to quickly move out.

If someone tries to cast this spell on you, you can break it by washing your doorstep twice a day, morning and night, for a couple of weeks until you no longer feel like you have to move.

Friendship Finale Spell

Sometimes a friendship is toxic and needs to end. You may have found out that one of your friends has been using you, or you may find that one of the people in your life is in a friendship that is bad for them. This spell burns the friendship up, then washes it away.

WHEN TO PERFORM THE SPELL

On a Saturday or during a Waning Gibbous moon

HOW LONG IT TAKES

20 minutes

WHAT YOU'LL NEED

- Wooden matches
- A wooden pencil
- A black candle
- A small piece of paper
- A heat-proof dish
- A river or stream

STEPS

1. Light the candle.

2. Write the name of the two friends who need to separate on the piece of paper. If you are one of the two friends, write your name on the paper as well as the other person's. Draw a circle around the two names.

3. Drop a bit of wax from your candle on top of the two names and visualize what you want to happen. Continue dripping wax until the circle is covered. Then say,

As is my will, this friendship will end
Two who were close will quickly defriend
As this spell is spoken
This friendship is broken.

4. Place the paper in the heat-proof dish and use the candle to light it on fire, allowing it to completely burn.

5. Let the candle burn out.

6. Take the ashes of the paper to a river and toss them in, and let the river carry the friendship away.

Courthouse Crossing

Courthouses are places of legal justice, but you can add a dash of magical justice to the proceedings with this spell. It will ensure that the judge in the case will see your target in the worst possible light. It won't guarantee a judgement for the side you favor, but it will nudge things in that direction.

WHEN TO PERFORM THE SPELL

On a Saturday or during a Last Quarter moon

HOW LONG IT TAKES

30 minutes

WHAT YOU'LL NEED

- A jar
- A photo of the person
- A piece of paper
- A pen
- Graveyard dirt
- Old string
- Vinegar – to sour the judge
- Black pepper – to make the proceeding painful
- Red pepper – to irritate the judge
- Black mustard seed – to cause confusion
- One lemon – also to sour the judge

STEPS

1. At the top of the piece of paper, write the person's name three times, one above the other.
2. Turn the paper 90 degrees and write the judge's name three times in the same way, crossing it over the target's name.
3. Lower on the paper, write,

This person deserves no second chance;
they have messed up too many times.
Do not be taken in by their song and dance;
Judge do not fall for their lies.
It is time for them to lose;
only you can make them pay their dues.

4. Place the paper and picture of the person in the jar, along with the black pepper, red pepper, black mustard seed, and graveyard dirt.
5. Add the old string to the jar next, to trip the target up in their court case.
6. Squeeze in juice from the lemon and fill up the jar with vinegar.
7. Place the lid on the jar and give it a good shake.

Shake it vigorously every day. On the day of the court case, give it an extra good shake. After the case goes to court, bury the jar somewhere far away from your house. Do not throw this jar away, because it could lead to the case being overturned.

Hole in the Head Hex

This spell is used to prevent someone from carrying out their plans, whatever they may be. The person you use it on will find themselves unable to focus enough to carry out anything complex

WHEN TO PERFORM THE SPELL

On a Saturday or during a Last Quarter moon

HOW LONG IT TAKES

15 minutes

WHAT YOU'LL NEED

- A picture of your target
- Sulfur wooden matches
- Salt – to weaken the target's will
- A needle

STEPS

1. Scrape the sulfur (the red part) from your match using your needle, creating a powder. Aside from just being flammable, sulfur is also used magically to harm enemies.
2. Sprinkle a pinch of salt over the picture of your target.
3. Sprinkle a pinch of the sulfur over the picture, focusing on the area around their forehead.
4. Using another match, light the sulfur and let it burn a hole in the area around the person's head. This will carry your

incantation to the mind of the target, ensuring that they are their own biggest enemy. Say,

Enemy of mine forever you will be
Your plans are all foiled no success will you see
No matter how hard you try, no matter what you do
No more success will ever come to you.

Do not allow the entire picture to burn up. If the fire gets bigger than a spot in the forehead, blow it out. Keep this picture on your altar until you are done with the spell, and then dispose of it.

Call the Law Spell

You can use this spell to bring protection to someone who needs it but can't, or won't, call for help themselves, or you can use it if the police have been called before but haven't responded appropriately. Using this spell will cause the police to turn up with a negative disposition towards anyone causing harm to the target of the spell, even if you make yourself the target.

This probably doesn't need to be mentioned, but just in case: if someone needs help immediately, call the police the mundane way.

WHEN TO PERFORM THE SPELL

On a Monday or during a Last Quarter moon

HOW LONG IT TAKES

15 minutes

WHAT YOU'LL NEED

- A white candle
- Anything representing the police (this could be a picture out of a magazine, for example)
- A picture of the person who needs to be protected
- Sandalwood oil – to make your wish come true
- Basil incense – to resolve the situation peacefully

STEPS

1. Anoint your candle with a few drops of sandalwood oil.

2. Light the incense as well as the candle

3. Place the picture of the police and the picture of the person who needs protection together, with the picture of the police on top. Say:

I call for protection for (the person's name) every day
When they are at (school/work) and when they play
I call for the police to come keep them safe
It's time to bring them some reason to have faith
No longer living in fear
I feel heroes are near.

As you speak the words, visualize the police showing up at the door of the home and rescuing whoever it is that needs to be rescued while arresting whoever it is that needs to be arrested. Visualize the happiness of the people who have suffered at the hands of their tormentor and visualize the tormentor finally being punished.

Mob Scene Jinx

If you find yourself up against a group of enemies, the best thing to do is to get them to fight among themselves. They may ignore you completely, or at least they'll be easier to deal with one on one.

I adopted this spell from one you read earlier. Remember, when you begin writing your own spells, you can mix things up and change them to fit your circumstances. You don't have to come up with completely new spells every time but can reuse old spells and change a few things.

WHEN TO PERFORM THE SPELL

On a Monday or during a Full moon

HOW LONG IT TAKES

45 minutes

WHAT YOU'LL NEED

- A knife
- A sheet of paper
- A jar
- A pen
- Scissors
- A shovel
- Vinegar – to sour the group
- Two lemons – also to sour the group
- Salt – to cleanse the group
- Red pepper – to irritate everyone in the group

- Black dog hairs
- Black cat hairs

STEPS

1. Write down on the paper all of the names of the people in the group, keeping them separate enough that you can cut them apart.
2. Cut out each name and fold them in half, placing them in the jar one at a time.
3. Carefully slice your lemons in half and squeeze all of the juice into the jar.
4. Sprinkle the salt over the paper and add in the red pepper.
5. Add in the black dog hair and the black cat hair. This will get them fighting like cats and dogs.
6. Pour the vinegar into the jar and shake well.
7. Take the jar outside and bury underground.

If you want to make the spell even stronger, you can pour vinegar over the spot every day and watch the group begin fighting nonstop.

Promise Keeper Binding

You may find yourself in the position of having to trust someone to keep a promise that you *know* has failed to do so in the past. Maybe it's a person at work you're depending on to deliver their part of a project, or a lover whose fidelity you want to ensure. Whatever the case, this spell will cause a person to keep their promises by causing them to feel pain whenever they consider doing otherwise.

WHEN TO PERFORM THE SPELL

On a Saturday or during a Full moon

HOW LONG IT TAKES

As long as it takes for the candle to burn out

WHAT YOU'LL NEED

- A tall purple candle
- A glass bottle (smaller than the candle)
- A sheet of paper
- A black pen
- Licorice root – for domination
- Calamus root – for control
- Knotweed root powder – to bind the person

STEPS

1. Turn the paper sideways and write the person's name in large print and then turn the paper 90 degrees clockwise.

2. Write down exactly what you want from your target. You may write down that you want them to keep their promise, but you should also include what that promise was.

3. Roll up the paper and insert it into the bottle.

4. Add the licorice root and the calamus root to the bottle.

5. Sprinkle s bit of knotweed root powder on the candle.

6. Place the candle in the bottle with the top of the candle sticking out, then light it. Say this,

A promise you made, a promise you did not keep
All your broken promises have cut me very deep
From this moment on, you will do what you say
When you think about breaking a promise, your life will
fall into disarray.
No promise will be made that you do not plan to keep
or only pain will you reap.

Allow the candle to burn out on its own. Do not dispose of the remnants of this spell until you are completely done with this spell.

Hard Luck Hex

Basil is often used in spells to increase luck, but for this spell we'll be using it like a sponge, to soak up the luck of the person you perform it on. Tying it to a rock grounds the energy of the person's luck the basil draws in, sending it down into the earth.

WHEN TO PERFORM THE SPELL

On a Sunday or during a Waxing Crescent moon

HOW LONG IT TAKES

20 minutes, then a three day wait

WHAT YOU'LL NEED

- A very rough rock about the size of the top of a bottle
- A slip of paper
- Black paint
- Bit of ribbon or string
- A dried bay leaf – to draw the luck away from the person

STEPS

1. Paint your rock black and allow it to dry.
2. Write the target's name on the slip of paper.
3. Place the paper on the rock, along with the bay leaf, and tie it all together with the ribbon.
4. Leave the rock for three days in an area that is very dark.

After three days, you will notice that the person is beginning to have bad luck.

14

A NASTY PIECE OF WORK

Our jobs can cause the majority of the stress in our lives, and the workplace is often where we can find the majority of our enemies. You can choose people you hang around with socially, but you're pretty much stuck with your coworkers...unless you have magic on your side.

This chapter is filled with simple spells that will ensure you can go to work every day and not worry about those people who constantly create drama.

Quitting Time Curse

We have all had coworkers who get on our very last nerve. Sometimes they are the bullies of the office, or they pick out one or two
people to focus on. Maybe they are your boss, or maybe they're the
person who refuses to carry their weight at work. This spell will
convince them it's in their own best interest to quit.

WHEN TO PERFORM THE SPELL

On a Wednesday or during a Waning Gibbous moon

HOW LONG IT TAKES

20 minutes

WHAT YOU'LL NEED

- ½ cup of olive oil
- A yellow candle
- The feather of a chicken – to cause rapid shifts in thought
- One teaspoon of salt – to purify the person right out of the office

STEPS

1. Light the candle
2. Add the salt to the olive oil.
3. With the chicken feather in one hand, say,

This is my time of need,

(person's name) must leave my place of work
For my own well-being and sanity, they must go
As the wheels set in motion (their name) will leave
And I will be free of them in my job
As I speak it, so will it be.

4. Dip the chicken feather into the olive oil.

5. Whenever you have the chance, take the feather and rub it across the floor where that person works.

Every time they cross over the mixture, the idea of quitting will pop into their head. If you an put it under where they sit, the idea will be on their mind constantly.

Enemy Eggshell Reveal Spell

If you think you have hidden enemies, it can be hard to know who to trust. Use this simple spell to compel people to show their true colors. For each person, you should use a separate.

WHEN TO PERFORM THE SPELL

On a Wednesday or during a Full moon

HOW LONG IT TAKES

20 minutes

WHAT YOU'LL NEED

- One egg for each person that you are concerned about
- A black marker
- A pot
- Cold water
- A stove

STEPS

1. Write the full names on each egg of the people that you suspect of being untrustworthy. One person per egg.
2. Carefully place the eggs in the pot and cover them with cold water.
3. Place the pot on the stove and bring the water to a boil. As you bring the water to a boil, say,

*The truth will no longer be hidden, bad eggs will crack,
enemies will now be seen.*

Continue to chant this as the water comes to a boil.

4. When the water has been boiling for about 60 seconds, turn
off the heat and place a lid on the pot. Set a timer for 15
minutes. When the timer goes off, check the eggs.

If any of the eggs are cracked, you should keep a close eye on the
person whose name is on that egg and be suspicious of their actions.
Their intentions will soon be revealed.

Job Preserving Oil

We live in a world where many people are without a job or cannot find a job that pays enough for them to live on. People are working two or three jobs just to make ends meet. So, when you find a good job, you want to make sure you keep it. When someone comes along thinking they will take your job, things can get tense.

This magic oil will protect your position, ensuring that it will be there for you in the long run and that no one will snatch it out from under you.

WHEN TO PERFORM THE SPELL

On a Wednesday or during a Waxing Crescent moon

HOW LONG IT TAKES

10 minutes

WHAT YOU'LL NEED

- Almond oil
- Allspice – to bring good luck to you
- Dill – to lower your enemy's chance of success
- Sage – for stability
- Cinnamon – to heat the work

STEPS

1. Place a pinch of each spice as well as the almond oil in a small bowl and mix well.
2. Store in a small dark-colored bottle.

Each day when you go to work, dab a bit of this on. Dab on a bit extra whenever you are near your boss or go to any meetings.

Promotion Jar Spell

Getting a promotion at work can seem as random as winning the lottery, especially if you know that someone else is up for it. To ensure that the promotion comes your way, instead of theirs, you can use this spell to tip the odds in your favor.

WHEN TO PERFORM THE SPELL

On a Sunday or during a Waxing Crescent moon

HOW LONG IT TAKES

20 minutes

WHAT YOU'LL NEED

- Olive oil
- Glass jar with lid
- 1 tbsp of grains of paradise – for success at work
- 1 tbsp of Cinnamon – to heat the spell and draw luck
- A key – to unlock the position

STEPS

1. Place the Grains of Paradise, cinnamon, and the key in the jar.
2. Fill the jar with olive oil.
3. Place the lid on the jar, and as you seal it, say,

As I seal this jar, I also seal my promotion.

4. Shake the jar vigorously.

Shake the jar daily until you receive your promotion. Once you have received your promotion, you may discard the remains of the spell.

Hire Me Spell

If you've ever been on a job hunt, you know that it often seems like you send out a hundred resumes without ever hearing a response. This spell causes your resume to float to the top, or the hiring manager to become interested in your application for a reason they won't really understand.

Make sure you've already applied for the job before starting this spell.

WHEN TO PERFORM THE SPELL

On a Wednesday or during a Waxing Crescent moon

HOW LONG IT TAKES

15 minutes

WHAT YOU'LL NEED

- A blue candle
- A large plate
- The job listing, printed out
- Peppermint leaves – to draw a job to you

STEPS

1. Place the blue candle in the center of the large plate.
2. Place the peppermint leaves in a circle around the candle.
3. Light the candle and read the job listing aloud seven times.
4. Light the job listing on fire and allow it to fall to the plate and burn completely up.

Leave the ashes on the plate until you get the results that you desire.

Get a Raise Spell

Maybe you don't want to get a promotion or change what you do at work, but you surely want to make more money. Use this spell to make that happen. This simple spell doesn't require an incantation, but do keep the desired results fixed strongly in your mind as you prepare it.

WHEN TO PERFORM THE SPELL

On a Sunday or during a Waxing Crescent moon

HOW LONG IT TAKES

10 minutes

WHAT YOU'LL NEED

- Shredded and dried ginger
- Walnuts
- Glass bottle with lid
- A hammer
- A towel

STEPS

1. Place your walnuts on the towel and crush them with the hammer.
2. Place the walnuts in the jar along with the dried ginger.
3. Place the lid on the bottle.

Hide the bottle until you get the raise, and only then should you dispose of the remains.

Workplace Sour Apple Curse

This spell will cause the person you perform it on to start making mistakes at work. The mistakes will start small but build over time as the apple used in it grows more and more rotten.

WHEN TO PERFORM THE SPELL

On a Monday or during a Dark moon

HOW LONG IT TAKES

30 minutes

WHAT YOU'LL NEED

- A red apple – always popular with wicked witches
- A knife to carve with
- Paper
- Wooden matches
- A pen
- A thick black candle
- A shovel to bury everything
- 1 tsp of poppy seeds – to make the target make mistakes
- Lemon juice and vinegar – to sour

STEPS

1. Carve the name of your target into the candle using the tip of your knife.
2. Light the candle.
3. Tear a small piece off of the paper and write the target's name on it. Also write on it something like "screw up at work".
4. Using the knife, cut a hole into the apple.
5. Place the paper into the hole.
6. Add a few poppy seeds to the hole.
7. Use the candle to drip wax into the hole until it is completely filled and sealed up.
8. Place your apple right next to your candle until the candle completely burns out.
9. Take the apple far from your home and dig a hole, placing the apple inside
10. Pour the lemon juice and vinegar on top and bury everything.

As the apple begins to rot, the target will begin making mistakes at work.

Presentation Fail Jinx

This spell is similar to the last one, but with a very specific form of mistake in mind. While the last one causes general mistakes, this one can be used when you want your target to make a very important, and very humiliating, mistake. It doesn't have to be failure during a presentation, you can specify the outcome when your write on the paper.

You will first create Commanding Oil. This oil can be used to get the person to do what you want them to do, in this case, fail during their presentation. You can use this oil in other spells as well; try it out and see how much fun you can have with it.

WHEN TO PERFORM THE SPELL

The Commanding Oil should be made during a Full moon. The spell itself should be cast on a Saturday or during a Dark moon.

HOW LONG IT TAKES

1 hour for the Commanding Oil. The spell will take as long as it takes the candles to burn out

WHAT YOU'LL NEED

For the Commanding Oil:

- Calamus root
- Licorice root
- Bergamot
- Vetiver

- Castor oil
- Mortar and pestle

For the spell:

- The Commanding Oil
- A black candle
- A white candle
- Three straight pins
- Paper
- A pen

STEPS

For the Commanding Oil:

1. Place all of the herbs into your mortar and pestle and crush them well.
2. Add them to the castor oil.
3. Heat the oil and herb mixture slowly until you start smelling the herbs.
4. Carefully pour the mixture into a dark-colored jar, ensuring that the herbs make it into the jar.
5. Allow this to sit overnight beneath the Full Moon.

For the spell:

1. Carve the target's name on the black candle and your name on the white candle.

2. Place the white candle, which represents you, above the black candle.

3. Anoint the black candle with the commanding oil.

4. Take your paper and pen and write down exactly what you want your target to do. Slip that paper under the black candle.

5. Insert the straight pins into the black candle starting about an inch from the top, making sure they are equidistant from each other.

6. Light both of the candles, the white one first and then the black one. Allow them to burn completely out.

As the candle burns and the pins begin to fall, your target will begin to lose their free will. After the candles have burned out on their own, bury all of the remnants.

Tower of Babel Curse

It's so hard to get people to communicate well, which makes a miscommunication spell fairly easy. You can use this to break apart two coworkers, or any two people, whose bond is in your way.

WHEN TO PERFORM THE SPELL

On a Wednesday or during a Waxing Crescent moon

HOW LONG IT TAKES

3 hours

WHAT YOU'LL NEED

- Two yellow tea candles
- A knife to carve with
- Jasmine oil – to confuse communication

STEPS

1. Anoint both candles with jasmine oil. Place them near each other.
2. Carve the name of the first person on one candle, and the second person's name on the other candle.
3. Light both candles, and say,

Spoken, but not heard,
Beseeched, but not understood,

Written, but not read,
The bond between you is dead.

4. Every 15 minutes for 3 hours move the candles two inches further apart. Allow the candles to burn out naturally.

Dominating Will Spell

Weakening a person's will is hard, so I suggest you don't try this spell until you've had success with several other spells in this book. It also requires some hard to get ingredients – the Commanding Oil used in an earlier spell, something personal from your target, and three drops of your own blood.

Even with all the work that goes into this spell, the outcome is that the person you perform it on will be more receptive to your suggestions or command, but they won't become a mental slave. And if you push too hard, they'll "wake up", breaking the spell.

WHEN TO PERFORM THE SPELL

On a Saturday or during a First Quarter moon.

HOW LONG IT TAKES

As long as it takes to burn down all three candles

WHAT YOU'LL NEED

- A picture of the target
- Some of the target's hair or an item that they have touched
- Three green candles
- Twine
- A pin
- Paper
- A pen
- Commanding Oil

STEPS

1. Write your target's name on the piece of paper.
2. Fold the paper at least three times but no more than seven times.
3. Use the twine to secure the paper to the person's personal item or their hair.
4. Anoint the candles with a few drops of Commanding Oil.
5. Prick your finger with the pin and add a drop of your blood to each of the candles.
6. Place the candles in a triangle around the person's personal item.
7. Light the first candle, when it burns out light the second, and when it burns out, light the third.

The person you perform this spell on will become more receptive to your control as the candles each burn down.

Pacify an Enemy

There are times when you have simply had enough, and all you want to do is pacify your enemy so that they will stop whatever it is that they are doing. When peace is all you want, there is a spell that can give you exactly that.

WHEN TO PERFORM THE SPELL

On a Saturday or during a First Quarter moon.

HOW LONG IT TAKES

As long as it takes to burn down all three candles

WHAT YOU'LL NEED

- Two purple candles
- A violet cloth
- A knife to carve with
- Wooden match
- Flat dish of salt – to purify the emotions between you both
- Lavender incense and lavender oil – to bring peace

STEPS

1. Carve your name into one of the purple candles and your target's name into the other.
2. Anoint each candle with a few drops of the lavender oil.
3. Spread out the violet cloth.
4. Place the two candles, the lavender incense, and the dish of salt on the cloth.
5. Light both candles and the incense.
6. Take a deep breath and breathe in the lavender. Calm your body, and using your finger, draw a pentacle into the salt. Repeat the following nine times,

Pacify my enemy now, no more fighting will I allow
This feud must come to an end
Although I do not want them to be my friend
It is time to have peace in my life starting right now.

7. Take a deep breath and visualize this person completely forgetting that you exist. See yourself living your life free of this person and in complete peace. Allow the candles to burn out on their own.

CONCLUSION

There was a time before I used spells that I suffered at the hands of other people. I thought that was how life was supposed to be. I believed that we just had to accept the hand that was dealt us, and there was nothing we could do about it. I hope that this book has taught you what it took me years to learn. You don't have to accept anything in life. You have the power to take control of your own life and to will it to be as you want it to be. You don't have to accept things from others that are painful, hurtful or distressing, and you have the power to get revenge if that is what you choose.

Many people who begin studying witchcraft do so because they have experienced some trauma in their lives. They turn to it because they are looking for help. They are looking for a way to take back control. What they usually find is talk of positivity or spells to heal other people. I know this is not what you were looking for when you started looking into witchcraft, which is why I wrote this book.

I shared my personal spells with you so that you can use them in your own life to begin talking to the dead and practicing divination. I want you to learn how you can use dolls in your spells and how knot magic can be used against people in your life.

I have always believed that it is vital for a witch to be able to cast spells that irritate and annoy those who upset them and to be able to practice relationship magic, as well as money magic. In my opinion, every witch needs to know how to deal with their enemies and do magic in the workplace.

It is crucial, however, that you do not forget the basics. Remember that there is no such thing as "black" or "white" magic." There is only magic. All of the information that you learned in Chapter 4 of this book about the phases of the moon, the seasons, and the colors are extremely important. If you want to be a powerful witch, memorize that information. Learn how to take care of your tools, as we covered in Chapter 2.

Remember that while spells are extremely fun and exciting, we also have to learn about the parts of magic that are not so fun. This will make us better, more powerful witches in the long run.

You're probably wondering, *Now what?* Maybe you have gone through this book and have cast the spells that were relevant to you, but there are some areas of your life that were left untouched. What should you do?

Well, you are never going to find a spell for every situation. However, I will tell you a secret. Someone had to write these spells, and now it is your turn. Get a sheet of paper and use all of the information that you learned in the first half of this book to start writing. If you need a refresher or you skipped right to the spells, go back. Take your time learning and try writing your own spells. I can promise you they will be the most powerful spells you have ever used.

CPSIA information can be obtained
at www.ICGtesting.com
Printed in the USA
LVHW051147210723
752798LV00050B/235

9 781736 656020